the secret of....

BOWLING STRIKES!

by DAWSON TAYLOR

With Photographs by Ray Glonka
Cover Photograph by Joe Clark

Published by
Melvin Powers
WILSHIRE BOOK COMPANY
12015 Sherman Road
No. Hollywood, California 91605
Telephone: (213) 875-1711 / (818) 983-1105

The Author

We are pleased to present what we believe is a most unusual book on bowling. The author of *The Secret of Bowling Strikes* is a forty-two-year-old automobile dealer in Detroit, Michigan. He is an amateur bowler who bowls twice a week in club leagues. He averaged 194 in the 1958 season and in the last three years has a cumulative average of 191 in the two leagues. And yet, in 1946, 1947 and 1948 he was a 165 average bowler!

In 1952, Dawson Taylor started analyzing "the secret of the strike ball." In 1958 his bowling record shows twenty-eight 200 games out of 75 league games with a strike average of almost five strikes per game.

Is there a "secret" method of throwing a strike ball? We really don't know, but perhaps Dawson Taylor has found one for himself and, we hope, for you, too!

—THE EDITORS

WHAT TO DO WHEN YOU ARE "IN TROUBLE"

Everyone runs into trouble occasionally in bowling, even the stars. All of a sudden, the ball that worked so well last week is jumping into the head pin leaving nothing but splits; or else it is failing to "come up" when you expect that it will and you find yourself missing usually easy spares.

What to do? The first thing is—don't get panicky and start to make radical changes. The first consideration is whether the difficulty lies in alley conditions or whether it is in your own ability to throw your usual type of delivery. Presume first that alley conditions are at fault and make your first correction by changing your "angle" as indicated in our earlier discussion on page 124. At the same time, without changing your delivery other than the slight change in starting position, line or spot, make sure that you are throwing a "live" ball, one with "action," as a result of the proper application of the "squeeze."

You may make a complete correction immediately and start scoring well at once. On the other hand, you may be in serious trouble and be faced with problems with both alley conditions and your own form, so that the corrections may not work right away or at all. You must realize that sometimes it will be impossible for you to make the necessary corrections and if that is so, reconcile yourself to a "bad night" and make the best of it. If you just can't get strikes, get every possible spare you can. If you are splitting frequently, try missing the head pin on the right (you'll find it hard to do) and then count your spare.

When every correction you can think of fails to work, make a radical change. If you have been bowling fairly close to the center of the lane, move away over to the corner. Do *something*, if only to help you to relax your tension.

Following is a check list compiled from asking star bowlers what they do when they get "in trouble." You should read it carefully and adopt the same procedure. This book is designed so that you can clip out this suggestion list and put it in your wallet. If you use it, it may save you many a bad night. Always try to have one of those "good" bad nights, one of those series when you escape with a respectable score when you know you shouldn't have!

CONTENTS

CHECK LIST FOR TROUBLE SHOOTING

1. I will check my starting position and my finishing position. Am I "drifting" right or left? Have I moved my start without realizing it?
2. Am I rushing the line? Are my hips square to the line at delivery point? Am I sliding straight?
3. Is my wrist firm with the thumb on the inside toward ten o'clock position? Is my grip secure, firm but relaxed?
4. Have I speeded the ball up or slowed it down without realizing it?
5. Am I releasing my thumb properly and is the ball going out over the foul line with the "squeeze" applied? Are my fingers clenched after the ball is delivered, or is my hand "open"?
6. Am I "pointing" the ball into the head pin, trying to put too much "stuff" on the ball?
7. Am I watching the ball go over its spot or line, or am I "pulling out" of the ball, pulling up and cutting short my follow-through?
8. Is my elbow wandering from my body causing a "side-arm" or "topping" of the ball?
9. Am I dropping the ball before I get it out over the foul line? Am I throwing it out too far over the foul line?
10. I resolve to be deliberate and take my time about each next delivery.

THE SQUEEZE

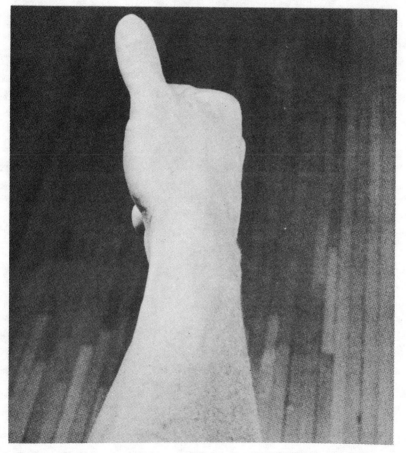

This is the SECRET of bowling strikes! SQUEEZE the ball at the explosion point!

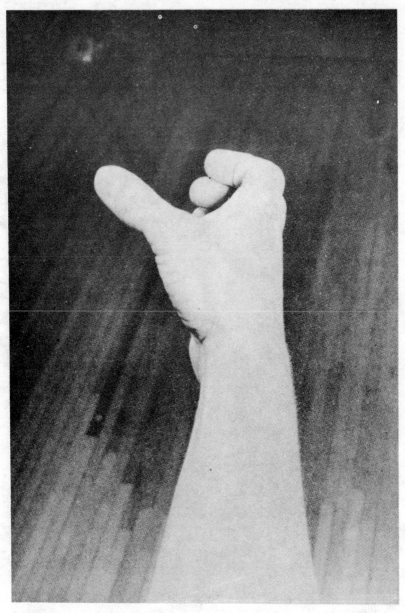

This is your beginning hand position, visualized without the bowling ball. Note the flat line of the back of the hand and forearm, the thumb pointing to "ten o'clock" position on a clock dial.

This is the same view but with the bowler's hand in the ball. The fingers are firm but relaxed. The wrist is firm. The hand is on the side of the ball with the thumb pointing to "ten o'clock." The left hand is helping to support the weight of the ball and is ready to drop away.

Another view of the beginning hand position. The white arrow on the ball should be visualized in actual play. It points to "ten o'clock." Your thumb inside the ball should be pointing on the same line as you look down at the ball.

This picture will help you to visualize your hand position at the "explosion point." If you could look down the instant before you begin to release your strike ball, you would find your hand and wrist in this position, ready for the SQUEEZE!

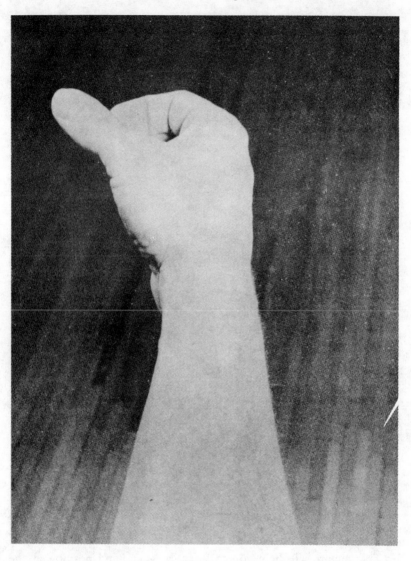

This is a view a fraction of a second after the SQUEEZE has started. Notice that the thumb has not changed its position. It remains relaxed and free. The fingers only are tensed and closing.

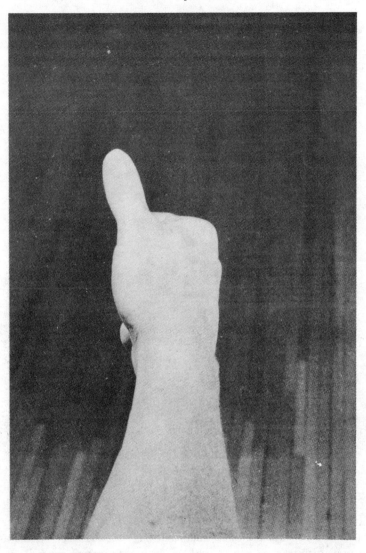

Now the SQUEEZE is completed. Note that the wrist position has remained the same, the flat line along the back of the hand and up the forearm. The thumb has moved slightly forward to what would be an "eleven o'clock" position of the clock dial. The thumb is still pointing to the inside of the body, to the left of the head pin.

Here's a close-up of the action the ball takes when the fingers SQUEEZE. Note that the hand and wrist have moved straight forward and upward; that the fingers, by their closing, squeezing the ball, have imparted the "turn" or rotation to the ball in a counterclockwise direction. Note that the arrow is disappearing around the side of the ball, indicating that while the ball is moving straight down the lane, or alley, it is "turning" counterclockwise.

Here is a view of the SQUEEZE completed and the noticeable action already starting on the ball. Notice that the thumb has moved forward to "eleven o'clock" position and the fingers are now clenched tightly together.

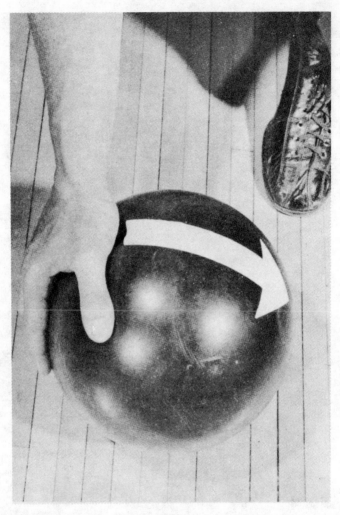

Now I want to show you the exercise you should practice in order to perfect yourself in this SQUEEZE action. First, place your ball in front of you near your left foot. Put your fingers only in the finger holes and let your thumb rest, relaxed, on the top of the ball. Try closing your fingers while they are in this position. You will find the ball wants to run away to the left.

After you have spun the ball many times without your thumb in the thumb hole, you may start to put your thumb part way into the ball. The thumb must remain very relaxed, without any tension in finger or forearm whatsoever.

Finally, you may place your thumb almost all the way into the thumb hole as you carry out this exercise. From the beginning of your practice, count the number of times you can make the ball revolve. You will find, at first, although it will be difficult for you to make it revolve one full revolution, that after much practice you can "drive" it around many times. More and more, you will achieve the finger sense of what must be done at the "explosion point," so that you will recognize the action.

THE EQUIPMENT FOR BOWLING

When you first start to bowl you will use a ball supplied by the bowling proprietor and perhaps even rented bowling shoes. Experiment for a while with the various weights of "house" balls. You will find that the weights vary from a minimum of 10 or 12 pounds up to the legal limit of 16 pounds.

If you are a big strong person you can, in all probability, handle the 16-pound ball. But, if you are on the small side, or if you are a woman, your bowling-ball weight should be less than 16 pounds, perhaps 3 pounds less. Even 6-ounce difference gives a noticeably lighter and easier-to-handle ball. In one of the "Classic" leagues, I know that there are many good bowlers who sacrifice that last half pound or pound in order to achieve greater accuracy and a lessened tendency to become fatigued.

By all means, as soon as you have decided that you like bowling and intend to continue to bowl regularly, get your own bowling ball, bag and shoes. Don't stint on the quality of your shoes because it is just as important to have proper-fitting shoes as it is for you to have a good-fitting bowling ball. Your bowling-ball grip should be snug but not too tight. Literally, it should "fit like a glove." You should have no trouble holding onto it in your backswing and yet it should release itself easily as your swing reaches its follow-through.

The various bowling equipment stores or bowling-lane proprietors will gladly measure and fit your hand and fingers to a bowling ball especially drilled for you, and once you have your own ball you will be much more prepared mentally to learn to use it well.

A complete kit, bowling ball, bag and shoes can be bought for less than fifty dollars; and when you consider the cost of equipping a golfer, for example, the price is extremely moderate. In fact, when you first buy your bowling ball, keep in mind the thought that perhaps this first ball will not be the one you will be eventually using. It is very difficult to get a ball that fits perfectly, and you will be sanding the various finger holes as you find abnormal wear on one or more of the fingers. It is most important that your thumb be able to "release" or get out of its finger hole easily; and yet a thumb hole that is too loose often causes a feeling of unease in the beginner bowler, who fears he may drop the ball in its backswing.

You may hear bowlers talking about the "pitch" in their bowling balls—so let's discuss it! "Pitch" means nothing more than the degree of inclination the finger holes have toward or away from the center of the bowling ball. The more the finger holes are cut in, so that the fingers can reach a curved or clenched position when they are placed in the ball, the greater the "grip" feeling the bowler has. But there is a point at which too much "pitch" or grip spoils the ability to get the fingers out of the ball, so by experimentation you will come to find the "grip" most suitable for you.

Most beginning bowlers seem to feel they are stuck with the ball they first buy. This is not so. Any ball can be filled, "plugged," they call it, and redrilled for very moderate cost. Remember that the ball must last leave your fingers somewhere and so you are bound to have some friction at that point. Bowling gloves are coming into vogue, and I personally advocate the use of a glove if your skin is at all soft and easily rubbed or blistered.

Be sure that your thumb is easily released and 90 per cent of your trouble will be over.

There are various types of patented "grips" on the market. I would advise you not to start out with one. Get a conventionally drilled three-finger ball with moderate pitch and learn to throw it and control it. Then, for a Christmas present, give yourself a new ball with a "trick" grip. However, don't give your old ball away. Maybe the new trick grip will help you to throw nothing but strikes and you may decide to keep it, or you may find that the "trickier" the grip the more difficult the bowling ball is to control and you will be glad you still have your old ball.

The star bowlers of today are throwing a "finger-tip" ball and they control it well by bowling ten to twenty-five games a day. Unless you can practice a great deal it is better that you stay with a conventional ball you can control.

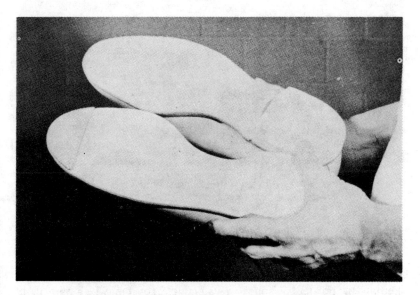

The "Odd" Construction of Bowling Shoes

Notice in the illustration above that the right-hand bowling shoe has a leather tip, rubber sole and heel, while the left-hand shoe has a smoother leather sole for sliding and a rubber "brake" heel. This will help to explain why the left knee must remain bent in its slide to the line, in order to keep the "brake" from being applied to the floor until the last moment after the delivery of the ball over the foul line. An abrupt straightening of the left knee will cause the "brake" to be applied too early and will result in a jerky, sudden stop. A left-hander's shoes are made in the opposite fashion.

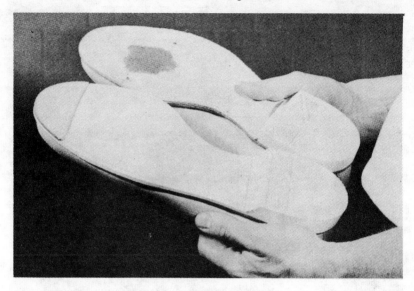

An Important Safety Tip

The left shoe in the illustration above has "picked up some water." Perhaps the bowler has gone to a water cooler, or it may be a rainy night and the various bowlers have been tracking in rain or snow onto the approaches. If a bowler makes his delivery not knowing that he has water on his left sliding shoe, he is apt to cause himself serious injury because the wet sole acts on the lane approach like a sudden brake. The bowler may foul unintentionally, may fall forward over the line, or even cause himself serious muscle strain. Good bowlers get in the habit of checking their sliding soles every time they bowl. Practice your slide at the front of the approach before you make your delivery. Doing this may save you a nasty spill.

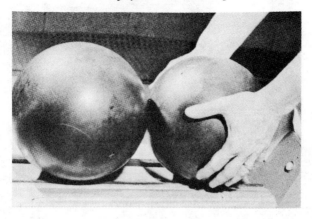

Right

These two illustrations show the right and the wrong way to pick a bowling ball from the rack. Always face forward and put each hand on the sides of the bowling ball. Don't put your hand between the balls on the rack, even if they are at rest, because an approaching ball can cause a chain reaction, strike your finger and perhaps break it. Another good suggestion is that you always lift the ball off and then support most of its weight in your left hand. In that way you will lessen the strain on your bowling hand and arm.

Wrong

THE ETIQUETTE OF BOWLING

The etiquette of bowling is based upon everyday rules of common politeness. If you are bowling on a team it is important to arrive at the bowling lane on time, and by all means, if you know you will be unable to bowl because of sickness or other good reason, call your captain and tell him in time to arrange for a substitute.

If you are bowling on a team and in a "match," even an informal one, it is polite to show enthusiasm for your team members' good bowling, their strikes, their difficult spare or split conversions. "Pep" and "chatter" on a team win more matches than you may realize. Once the team that is a great number of "marks" behind, halfway through the game, begins to chop away at the deficit, the leading team starts to try harder, and invariably loses some of its lead and often is squeezed out in the tenth frame. So be enthusiastic even when the tide rolls against you and your team.

Some of the niceties and fine points in bowling the individual game are based upon sensible rules. The main rule is that the bowler, right or left, who has his spare to shoot, has the right of way over the bowler who has a full setup or ten pins to knock down. So defer to your opponent who has his second ball to roll. Should he motion you to go ahead anyway, you are perfectly free to do so. He may want another minute or so to contemplate his spare.

There is an unwritten rule that if a bowler on a pair of lanes has a split left standing, he will immediately clear it away so that the bowler with the full setup does not have to "look at it" while bowling his first ball.

When both bowlers are rolling first balls, or each one is bowling at a spare, the bowler on the right has the "honor" to proceed. Sometimes the presence of other bowlers on other nearby alleys will cause a bowler some distraction, so he will motion to his opponent to go ahead. Use good sense and you'll be right most of the time.

Just as in football or baseball, a good sport congratulates his opponent on his strikes and good conversions. It is highly improper to "needle" an opponent or an opposing team with taunts or comments on misses or splits. The best way to upset an opponent or an opposing team is to get a fine string of strikes for yourself or your team.

It is most important for each bowler to realize that usually he and he alone is interested in how well or how badly he bowls. Consequently, exhibitions of temper of complaints about alley conditions or "luck" are in extremely bad taste. Remember that good luck usually is counterbalanced by bad luck, and when you have a run of bad luck, be patient. Sooner or later, perhaps even the next time you bowl, you will get that lucky hit in between two strikes so that you can "steal a triple," or three strikes in a row.

For the very same reason—self-interest in bowling—do *not* offer free advice to any bowler before he asks for it. One of the top bowling teams in the country has a strict rule that no one is allowed to make a suggestion to another team member without permission of the team captain, and he rarely does so except in extreme necessity. The reason for this rule, which should be observed by all team bowlers, is that the bowler who is bowling badly becomes more confused than ever when criticism or suggestion for correction is offered. First, he has already probably made several attempts at correcting himself, and on top of his own correction will come perhaps a radically different one. There are many ways to correct a bowler, by slowing him down, by speeding him up, by moving him one way or the other, etc., and possibly the offered correction is entirely wrong. The best advice, if advice must be given, is "Take your time," which really is more of a psychological correction, good no matter what he is doing wrong.

A most important rule concerning the "etiquette of bowling" is that you should *never* pick up your ball from the rack while another bowler is preparing to throw his ball down the next alley. This is extremely distracting to the bowler and you will feel as bad as he does when he delivers a "bad" ball.

THE SCORING MARKS IN BOWLING

Bowling is scored by "marks" which are very distinctive. There are ten "frames" in each game and each one has a little square in its upper right corner and looks like this:

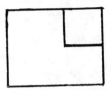

The upper right-hand square is used to indicate whether or not the bowler:

1. Knocked all ten pins down in his first ball with a "strike," which would be scored:

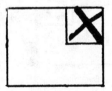

2. Knocked all ten pins down in two balls for a "spare," which would be scored:

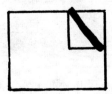

3. Or did not knock down all ten pins in either of two balls, thus scoring a "miss," or "open frame," which would be scored:

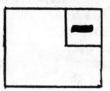

And, as if to take the sting out of an "open" frame which is the result of a split, the early bowlers devised a symbol to show that the bowler really couldn't help not knocking them all down in two tries because they were too far apart. The scoring mark is:

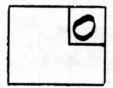

Once in a while when a bowler "makes a split" or knocks down the separated pins with his second ball, the split mark "O" is crossed through with the spare mark "/" and the bowler rejoices at "filling" what appeared to be an "open frame" with a

Another interesting mark you will run across is a "c," which is sometimes used to indicate a missed spare where there are originally two pins close together, such as in the 6–10 spare, and the bowler in attempting to make the spare "chops" off one or the other of the two pins.

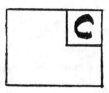

Sometimes when you are watching a bowling match, either individual or team, you will see the scorekeeper keeping a numbered tally between the scoring lines and, frame by frame, it may look something like this:

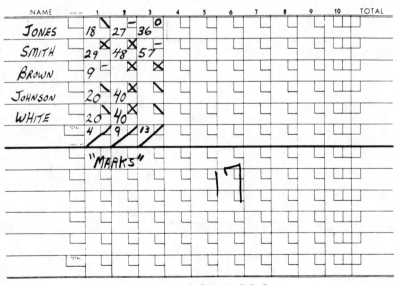

D·A·C BOWLERS

This indicates the total number of strikes and spares, cumulatively from the first frame through the ninth. Each spare or strike of a team member counts one "mark," or approximately ten pins. By totaling "marks" frame by frame the over-all scoring position can be determined fairly accurately.

When one team is "spotted" a certain number of pins so as to handicap the better team, the marks are usually added in either the first frame or else at random throughout the game, as if a phantom bowler were coming up with crucial "marks" when the team most needed them.

Once in a while you'll hear the expression, "take a mark off," by which you'll know a bowler has just had a very bad "count," four pins or less on a spare or strike, and thus has cost his team ten pins. And, as a matter of interest, you'll always hear the remark from the opponents' team, not from your own side.

THE LANGUAGE OF BOWLING

Bowling has a pleasant jargon of its own and if you understand it well you will find that you can join the crowd in cheering, criticizing the bowlers around you; and "knowing the language," you will be so much more a part of the great game.

Most bowling terms seem to describe various types of bowling-ball "action," and rather than compile a dictionary, word for word for you, it is my belief that there is a better way to do it. So here goes!

You have entered the bowling lane and if one of your teammates laughingly tells you as you put your bowling bag down, "Don't get that water all over me!" he's merely referring to your bad night last week when you were throwing a "water ball," "pumpkin," a "flat one," or a "tomato."

You proceed to bowl and your first ball is a slow curve that just barely comes up to the head pin, but once it touches it, all the pins start to dance and tumble down for a strike. Someone calls and says "You pulled the rug out from under that one!" or "You really stole that one," or "You're not going to take that strike, are you?" And soon after, getting up a little speed, you throw a strike on a ball that normally you expect to hook into or across the head pin, but it does not, and holds a direct line, and at the last moment seems to "set" and drives high and hard on the head pin for a strike. You come back to the bench and say, "Boy, was that a tight one! I was a little scared until it 'set'!" or, if all the pins flew backward straight into the pit without any question of doubt, you might say, "Was that a crasher!"

A "solid" hit is one right in the 1–3 pocket with such force and authority that usually a strike results. So it follows that a "solid 10 pin" is one that is left standing after a "solid" smash. Don't be ashamed of "taps," that is, leaving a 10 pin or a 4 pin or a 7 pin on what appears to be a good hit. A pin off-spot a fraction of an inch one way or the other, or erratic ball action at the last moment, can cause strange pin action and the loss of a strike that you might normally expect. Take your time and concentrate on converting the single-pin spare, for all too many lone pins are missed merely because the bowler "blows the spare"—still rankling over the injustice of having left the single pin stranded on a good hit and forgetting to concentrate.

When you get your second strike in a row, you have "doubled"; you are now "working on a big one." And when you get your third strike in a row you have a "turkey," or "triple." More strikes in a row give you a "string" of strikes—one of the pleasures of bowling, especially when you get a lucky "Brooklyn" or "Jersey" hit in the opposite pocket, the 1–2 instead of the 1–3. And you will have more groans from the enemy and more encouragement from your own team as they say, "Don't be embarrassed, take it and sit down!"

And then come the splits! The "baby splits" are the 3–10, which a right-handed bowler draws frequently on a "high" hit, one that goes into the head pin too much toward the center; and the 2–7, usually drawn by the left-hander. The nasty 4–6, 7–10, the two pins on each far side of the lane, is called variously "double pinochle," the "Big Four," or just plain "Ugh!" The 8–10 is called a "strike split" because it results from what seems to be a good 1–3 pocket hit. No matter what it is called, it's one of the impossibles.

Lanes, or alleys, are "running" when you can't hold your ball off the head pin; "stiff" when you can't make your ball curve and "come up" to the head pin. They are "soft" lanes when you regularly score well on them; "rough" or "tough" or "mean" when they are hard to score on.

And there are a thousand more words and phrases you needn't know now. You'll learn them as you go along, and perhaps even invent a new one!

THE SCORING IN BOWLING

or

HOW TO ADD BY 10's

Every beginning bowler seems to think that scoring in bowling is difficult to understand. Many bowlers grow panicky when the job of scorekeeper is suddenly thrust upon them. In many leagues it is customary for the captain to be the scorekeeper, and consequently it is very important that you learn to score properly. There are some tricks to it, it must be admitted, but once you know the basis for scoring and find that you can do it correctly, there is a great deal of satisfaction in having a well-written score sheet, accurately kept. Your teammates, while they may not say it in so many words, will genuinely appreciate your talent.

The "secret" of scoring in bowling will astound you. You don't add; you *subtract*. Strange as this statement may seem, it is the "trick" that makes good scorekeepers.

At least half the time (or more, if you become a really good bowler) you will be "working on the spare." This means that you will be adding a "bonus" of 10 to the number of pins knocked down on the first ball of the next frame. And here is where the secret comes in: instead of adding 10, add 20 and subtract the number of pins you have left standing.

Example: "Working on a spare" with 27 in the second frame, you knock down 8 pins. Addition method—10 + 8 = 18, to be added to the score of the previous frame; 27 + 18 = 45 and the mathematical steps were difficult, weren't they? Now let's try the "trick" way: 27 + 20 = 47 (It's easy to add by 10's or 20's) and take away the 2 pins left standing. Answer: 45. Simple, isn't it?

All the discussion about how difficult it is to score in bowling, I am convinced, is a result of the natural inability of most people to add their 7's and 8's and 9's, which occur quite often if you add in the old-fashioned way. The other way, the "trick" method, makes it much simpler for you, and once you get the hang of it you'll find scorekeeping easy to do. Always remember to ask yourself: "How many pins are left standing?" And you have your answer, whether the bowler has a miss, a spare or a strike.

Now let me show you that this system works equally well on splits, misses or strikes.

There are four simple basic situations to understand:

1. If the bowler does not knock down all the pins in two balls, immediately total the number knocked down. By the "trick" method, in your mind add 10 and take away the number of pins left standing.

2. The spare situation we have just covered.

3. On a strike, you will add to the next two balls the bowler rolls. If the bowler spares in his next frame by knocking down all the pins in two balls, add 10 and 10 for a total of 20. And this immediately suggests that you now learn that

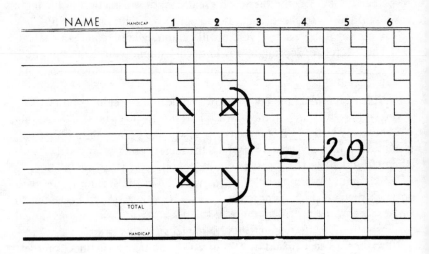

spare-strike or strike-spare always means a 20 count added to the first frame, whether spare or strike:

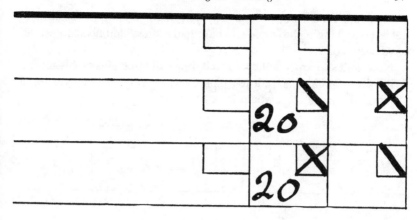

4. The tenth frame is the only unusual frame in bowling scoring. If the bowler scores a strike or spare in his tenth frame he throws a third ball for additional "count."

So remember that scoring after a strike is 10 added to the next *two* balls and scoring after a spare is 10 added to the next *one* ball. And, if all ten pins are *not* knocked down in one or two tries, the total number of pins knocked down is entered on the score sheet.

Now, let's score an imaginary bowler for a few frames and see how really simple it is.

Jones bowls his first ball in his first frame and knocks down seven pins. You do not score a total until you see whether he knocks down the three remaining pins on his second ball. Jones misses the three remaining pins. He has scored a "miss" and his first frame will show:

JONES   7 ⁻

If he had knocked down one or two of the remaining three pins and yet left one standing he would still have had a "miss" but his score would have been 8 or 9.

Now, let's suppose that he knocked down all three pins on his second ball, which would mean all ten pins down on two balls, or scoring a "spare." His score sheet would look like this:

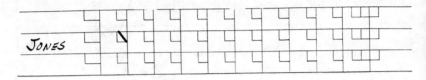

No score is entered because the scorekeeper must wait to see how many pins Jones knocks down on his next ball, which is the first ball of the second frame.

Jones proceeds to throw the first ball of his second frame and knocks down eight pins, leaving two standing. The scorekeeper adds 10 (the scoring bonus for sparing) to 8, the number of pins on the first ball, and then enters 18 in Jones' first frame.

Jones bowls the second ball of his second frame and misses, leaving the two pins standing. His score is totaled forthwith—18 on the first frame plus the 8 knocked down in the second frame. His score looks like this:

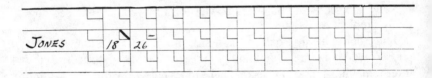

Note that a "miss" is indicated in the second frame.

Jones proceeds to strike in his third frame, knocks all ten pins down with his first ball. His score sheet now shows:

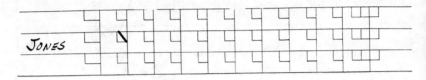

Let's let Jones spare in his fourth frame and strike again in his fifth. Remember: Strike-spare or spare-strike means 20 count, so here's how you score him:

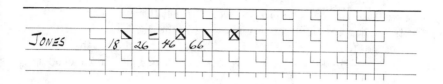

Frame number five remains open until Jones has bowled two more balls. This time he's a hero and strikes each time in frames six and seven. His score now looks like this:

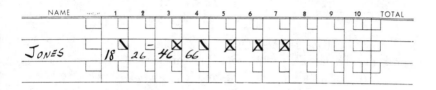

On a "string of strikes," bowling superstition says, "Don't score anything until the string is broken." Actually, when you are ready to score for him in the fifth frame, Jones has earned 30 pins, the 10 bonus plus the total of his next two balls (each 10). So in your mind's eye score him 66 + 30, or 96, in the fifth and wait to see what he does in his eighth frame.

In his eighth frame he draws a wide-open split, the 8–10, and counts one of those pins, the 10 pin. It's an "open" frame, so you score right through the open frame.

To get Jones' score in the sixth frame you add 10 to his next two balls, which were a strike (10) and 8, the first ball of the eighth frame. Or, by the "trick" method on a "double," add 30 and take away the pins standing after the first ball.

For his seventh frame, you see that he had a "strike up," meaning "wait for two balls before you score." Jones threw two balls in the 8th frame and counted nine. So, his score in the 7th frame is now 10 + 9 (or the "trick" way 20 − 1), for 143; and since he did not spare or strike in the eighth, you fill in his score, adding the nine pins he knocked down in the eighth, for 152.

We'll let Jones strike out in the ninth and tenth for a "full count"; each time he will earn 10 plus the total of his next two balls (10 plus 10), or 30, so his score will look like this:

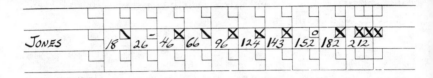

And you have learned a great deal about scoring. Now for some practical advice, especially useful for team scoring. You will have two bowlers "up" at a time on right- and left-hand alleys. Get the habit of seeing what each bowler has "up" in his previous frame. If one has a spare and the other a strike you know you have to watch the spare-bowler's first ball but will wait for two balls from the strike-bowler. If one of them is working on a double, be ready to score him through a split or miss with his 30 count, less what pins are left standing—and, above all, be vigilant. Pay attention to your job, for there's nothing more annoying to both bowler and scorekeeper to hear the question asked, "What did you do in the last frame?"

Your fellow bowlers will love you if you can tell them, "Get a full count for two-oh-four!" and you will if you can learn to score the "trick" way, shown here.

THE STRATEGY OF BOWLING

As in most sports, the purpose of bowling is to attain as high a score as possible. Therefore, it is useful to consider various situations which can affect your score favorably or unfavorably and understand the strategy which should be employed when you encounter them.

Most important is the decision of how to bowl against splits. In the discussion in the chapter on scoring, you will remember that the scoring after a strike is the total of the next two balls. So if you happen to draw a split after a strike or leave a large cluster of pins, not a split, be certain to "count" or knock down as many pins as possible because each extra pin knocked down counts as two. For example, the bowler leaves two pins on the right-hand side and one on the left in the 6–7–10 split. He has had a strike in the previous frame. If he knocks down the two pins on the right he will count 19 plus 9—28, whereas if he knocks only the number 7 pin down or only one of the 6–10 combination he will score 18 plus 8–26, or two fewer pins.

In general, always be careful after a strike and do your very best to strike again or at least "hit the pocket" (the number 1 and 3 for right hand bowlers) so that you can take advantage of the "count" in a strike.

Sometimes when the entire result of a team game is so close that the conversion of a wide-open split might make the difference between winning and losing, the good bowler will often try to "convert" or make the split. Wide-open splits that can be attempted with some hope of converting are those in which at least one pin is on a line in front of the other or others, offering the opportunity for the ball to clip the front on one side and slide it across to knock out the other pin or pins. Study the photographs and analyses of the best ways to convert typical splits and spares and you will understand better the technique involved in converting them.

A conversion of a difficult spare when your team most needs the pins is one of the high points of bowling, one of the "thrills of a lifetime" that you and your teammates will talk about for years to come.

You should understand the importance of "ninth frame" strategy. This means that, if at all possible, you should "lay a foundation" for your tenth frame by getting a strike in your ninth frame. It is a very relaxing feeling to know that you have "one to work on" in the tenth, not only because of the advantage of additional "count" on any strike but also because of the chance that you may "strike out" in the tenth, put three more strikes together and "get a full count."

Let's take two bowlers, Smith and Jones, with identical scores in the eighth frame, say 165, and let Smith have a spare in the ninth and Jones a strike in the ninth. Their scores look like this:

| | SMITH | 165 | — (9th: spare) | | |
| JONES | 165 | X (9th: strike) | | |

Now, let each bowler "strike out" in the tenth frame and their scores look like this:

NAME	HANDICAP	1	2	3	4	5	6	7	8	9	10	TOTAL
SMITH									165	185	215	
JONES									165	195	225	

Or, let each bowler spare in the tenth, with nine pins on the first ball and a conversion of his one-pin spare to "close the frame." Then their scores will show:

NAME	HANDICAP	1	2	3	4	5	6	7	8	9	10	TOTAL
SMITH									165	184	204	
JONES									165	185	205	

Which shows so clearly how important it was for Jones to have gotten his strike in the ninth. Either way, he has counted more pins than his opponent who was "working on a spare." So watch the top bowlers in their ninth frames! They all try their hardest to get that ninth-frame strike!

TAKING ADVANTAGE OF THE "ANGLE"

The more you contemplate bowling, the more you realize that it is a rather tantalizing game. No sooner does the bowler knock down the pins than presto! they are all set up again as if in defiance, saying "Well, you did it once, maybe, but you can't do it again!"

It is extremely important that the bowler understand the mathematics of bowling so that he can take advantage of every chance to knock down the greatest number of pins.

The first thing to understand is the obvious disparity in requiring a round ball weighing 16 pounds or less to roll down an alley bed of hardwood some 62 feet long and by striking against the first two of ten pins, each weighing up to 4 pounds, knock them all down at once.

Notice that you are asking a 16-pound ball to knock down up to 40 pounds of wood! There is a trick to this. *Angle!* The pins are set up in a triangular formation like this:

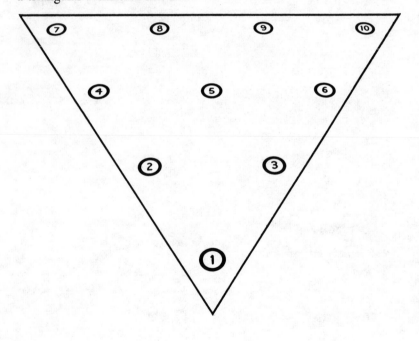

The kingpin is not, as you might think, the headpin (1). It is the 5 pin! And with good reason is it called the kingpin. For, when you can put your first ball into the pin setup and knock down the 5, its tumbling impact on the other pins helps to cause the "action" which may or may not result in a strike.

The second very important mathematical fact that must be considered is "deflection" of the bowling ball as it strikes the pins. You have probably seen an automobile skid on an icy pavement, strike a curb and bounce off. Exactly the same thing happens when the 16-pound (or less) bowling ball strikes first one pin and then another.

So, a little bit later on when you look at the diagrams and read the discussion of the best way to make a strike, a spare or a split, you will better understand why it is advised that the ball be rolled from one "angle" or another. You will be taking advantage not only of the lessened chance that deflection will cause you to miss a second or third pin, but also you will be using the width of the ball itself to help cut a swath through the pins.

Besides the physical fact of the mass and velocity of the bowling ball affecting "deflection," the weight of the pins is important. Not for anything other than interest, it is quite revealing to contemplate that a ladies' 12-pound ball striking against 3-pound, 6-ounce bowling pins must exert 42 per cent more energy to equal the force of a man's 16-pound ball against so-called "lightwood" of 3 pounds 2 ounces.

But each ball is some 9 inches wide, and it is obvious that if any part of its 9-inch-wide track touches a pin it will most probably knock that pin down. Since the middle of the pin is 4¾ inches wide, it is evident that in order to miss a one-pin spare in the middle of the alley it is necessary to miss a target about 23 inches wide, the combined total of two pin widths plus the ball width. So you know now why some bowlers say, "You should *never* miss a one-pin spare!"

THE FUNDAMENTALS OF BOWLING

Now let's review a few bowling fundamentals so that you will reach the foul line in the proper body position to SQUEEZE the ball.

In my opinion, there are four major fundamentals of bowling. These are RELAXATION, TIMING, LINE, and SQUARENESS.

First, you must learn to relax in order to bowl your best. In tournament competition or even close league competition this is difficult for all bowlers to accomplish. If you follow these simple suggestions, you will be more relaxed and, knowing that you are, you will bowl better.

About relaxing your grip: Slap the ball or pat it as if it were a baby just before you insert your fingers into the finger holes. Always place your fingers in their holes first, and then the thumb. This practice helps to keep you aware of the need for the finger action explained elsewhere. It will also rid you of the fear that your thumb is "buried" in its thumb hole. Many good bowlers can be seen practicing their thumb release as they prepare to throw their strike ball.

Your wrist must be firm, not loose. You should feel the firmness in the outside of your arm and along the straight line from the back of your hand past your wrist and up your forearm. I will explain this anatomically a little later on. Your arm is definitely looser than your wrist. In fact, one great bowler has described his bowling arm as "limp as a dishrag" when he is bowling his best.

Now, about bodily relaxation: Break your knees slightly at your beginning bowling position. Take a tip from the great Ben Hogan and "sit down" a bit. Before you make up your mind to start your push-out, look left and right to make sure that no other bowler is going to disturb your concentration. Don't ever step into your bowling position until you are mentally certain, and therefore relaxed about it, that no other bowler is going to upset your concentration by picking up his ball from the rack, by bodily gyrations at a nearby line, or by any other distraction. Thus, you are assured of a relaxed delivery free of disturbances.

Now that you are ready to bowl, take a good deep breath. Hold it slightly, and then slowly exhale. Then just as you complete the exhalation, go! You will find that you cannot be tense immediately after the exhalation of a deep breath. This tip alone will save you much anguish in tournament bowling.

Let's talk a bit about the second fundamental—TIMING. Don't rush the line. Take your first step slowly, and gradually increase your speed until you come to the foul line. A top bowler once said, "Take your SECOND step slowly and then you will *have* to take your first step slow!" It's good advice.

Work on timing your pushaway. Whether you start the ball waist-high or chest-high, or throw it way up in the air as the great Don Carter does, time your pushaway so that when you reach the foul line, sliding smoothly with your left foot, the ball and arm are just passing your left foot. If you have a four-step delivery—and most good bowlers do—make your push coincide exactly with your first step. If you find that you are getting to the line too soon with the ball, lengthen your pushaway by starting it higher. If you are there too late, shorten it by starting it lower. Remember, too, that your pushaway can be speeded up by an actual *push* down as you start the ball away from your body into its backswing. In general, the same rules prevail for speeding up or slowing down the bowling arc for three- or five-step bowlers. No matter how many steps you take, you must time your last several and your slide so that arm and ball are just passing your left heel at the "explosion point" of your delivery.

In working on your timing, I strongly suggest that you adopt a timing exercise which you can do at home (see the chapter on "How to Practice Bowling Away from the Lane"). A metronome can be purchased for about $5. This investment will pay dividends many times over in your bowling success and pleasure.

THE PRACTICAL APPLICATION OF THE FUNDAMENTALS

On most modern lanes, or alleys, just short of the "break of the boards," which can be seen here to the left of the picture, there are arrow-like markers installed in the alley bed. These markers should be used to line up your bowling delivery. Before you throw your first bowling ball of the day, pick out one particular board between the second and third markers from the right-hand side of the lane, and from your starting position draw on the lane your imaginary "line." Your left foot should be used as your "pointer" and always placed on the same dot in the approach. This beginning "dot" will be somewhere near the center of the alley and will depend upon your ability to put "action" on the ball.

Always start from the same position and throw over the same board at the "break of the boards," down the same line until you have had an opportunity to observe whether your normal ball is hitting the pocket. Then, if any adjustment is necessary, a good rule to follow is, "Always move with your error," which means that if your ball is crossing too high on the headpin or to the left, you will move your starting position to the left. If you move to the left, your ball will tend to go farther to the right and should come into the pocket in better position. Never move your starting position more than half a board or a board at a time, and always keep accurate mental track of your last starting position or else you will become hopelessly confused. The reverse strategy usually works when your ball is not coming up to the headpin, or is missing on the right. Move your beginning position slightly to the right, keeping your normal "spot" between the markers as the pivot point between approach and the pins.

You have located your spot on the approach with your left foot. Your right shoulder is directly in line with the "line" you intend to throw down. You are sighting the imaginary line. Your knees are slightly bent and your weight is back on your right heel.

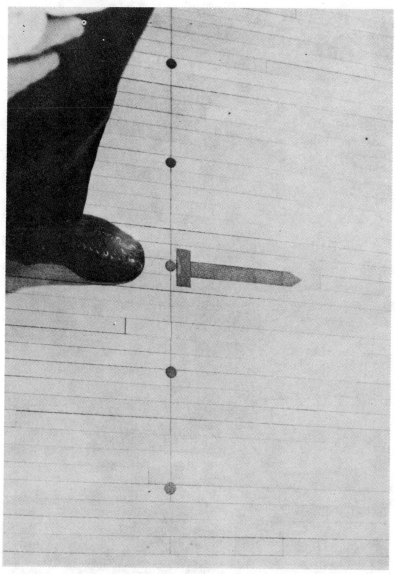

You have carefully placed your left toe on the marker at the center of the lane. Your right foot and right shoulder are in line with one of the boards about a foot to the right of the center of the lane. This is your imaginary line and you will attempt to roll the ball directly down that line.

This is the moment of the pushaway. At *exactly* the same instant that you push the ball forward into its arc, your right foot moves into its first step. If this action is consistently timed to coincide precisely, 90 per cent of your troubles in timing are solved.

You are into your second step. The ball is dropping into the back-swing and your right foot is making its move straight down the imaginary line. Note that the hand position has not changed in relation to the body since the first moment of the pushaway. It will not change throughout the entire bowling swing!

This is the point at which your ball begins to return in the downswing. Note that your hand position has not changed. The thumb is pointed to the inside, the back of the hand and wrist are still flat. Do not try to hurry this downswing as you may turn your hand one way or the other and cause error in "overturning" the ball, which means that the ball is spun off the thumb without the proper "squeeze" at the explosion point.

Here is a view showing the hand position at the "explosion point" from head-on. Note that the thumb is still pointed to the inside, the flat wrist and back of the hand, the closeness of the arm in its swing beside the left instep, the straight-on slide of the left foot as it slides into the exactly corresponding dot from which it started at the beginning of the approach.

Here is the "explosion point" a fraction of a second after the SQUEEZE has been imparted to the ball. The fingers have not yet had time to close completely. The ball is slightly lofted out onto the lane, traveling about an inch above the boards anywhere from 6 inches to a foot and a half before it will touch down onto the "line." Note the left foot still sliding toward its designated "dot" target on the approach.

Here is a view of the finish with the right hand having come up clenched, thumb still inside, straight forward with the line of the ball. Note the balance evident in the position of the right foot and the left arm—the left knee still bent and sliding into the final stop position. Note, too, the intense concentration with the eyes still watching the "spot" on the boards at the "break of the boards." The right shoulder has definitely followed through with the bowling swing.

Here is another view of the follow-through absolutely necessary in order to throw a strike ball. The thumb is clearly still on the inside and the back of the hand and wrist are still "flat." "Squareness" to the line is very clear in the hips and, in general, in the attitude of the entire body. (The bowling ball in every action picture was actually bowled. There were no "posed" action pictures whatsoever.)

HOW TO PRACTICE BOWLING
AWAY FROM THE LANE

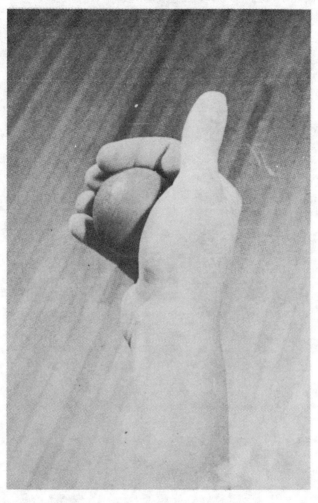

This is a view of the rubber-ball squeezing exercise you should carry out from ten to twenty times each day. Get a rubber ball small enough to fit your hand in the beginning clenched position of your bowling grip and practice squeezing it with the thumb relaxed, energizing only the muscles which activate your last three fingers.

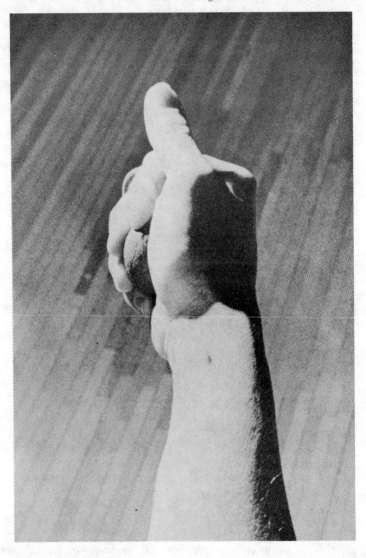

This is the view of the clenched third, fourth and fifth fingers around the rubber ball after the SQUEEZE has been accomplished. This motion of the fingers should be sudden, and the fingers should be held tightly in the clenched position after the action is done. The muscles on the inside of the arm should be tense, holding the fingers in closed position. The thumb should be completely free and relaxed and pointing to the "eleven o'clock" position.

Here is your exercise to train you for a perfectly straight approach: Take a large roll of one-inch-wide white adhesive tape and lay it down in a straight line about 10 feet long on a floor at home. With your hands on your hips, practice walking this line from your normal beginning bowling stance, placing your right foot on the right side of the line and your left foot on the left side. Keep your eyes on the line all the time. Bend your left knee and slide on your last step, taking care to slide perfectly straight forward. Use some dance-floor wax if you need it.

After you have practiced walking the line for a matter of hours, you will find that the white line is impressed in your mind so sharply that you can see it even with your eyes closed. This line should be so burned into your mind's eye that from now on you will be able to see it on every bowling approach you make. You may now set your metronome to the tempo you wish to hold. Bowl with your imaginary bowling ball for a long time before you attempt to work with your ball on the practice line.

Obviously, you cannot "bowl" at home, but you can accustom yourself to the rhythm of the metronome by swinging the bowling ball gently in its arc even though the arc is shortened of necessity. Remembering your rules of physics, the pendulum motion of the ball takes just as long for a short arc as for the long arc which you will employ in actual play. Work with the metronome and concentrate on keeping your hand position correct.

When you can walk the line fairly straight, with the right foot on one side of the line and the left on the other, then start practicing your slide on the last step. Bend your knee and you will discover that the brake (the left heel of rubber) on your bowling shoe does not touch the floor until your knee straightens. Also, you will find that while your knee is bent you can reach out over the imaginary line much farther than if you straighten your left knee and lock it as you come to the line.

When you bowl in practice in a bowling alley, you should disregard your score at least half the time. Thinking about scoring, you may forget to concentrate on the proper hand action you should be using and get back into bad habits. As you develop your strike ball, you will find that your pin "leaves" are more and more frequently single pins instead of the clusters you have left in the past. Besides, with your stronger ball you will find that you are removing that troublesome number 5 pin and, as a result, you are no longer getting many splits with the 5 pin as one of the setup. The same thing will hold true of the 8 pin. Time after time you will see the 8 pin fall out of an 8–10 potential leave and you will then realize that it was the strength of your ball that got through and knocked out the number 8 to leave you the simple one-pin spare, the 10 pin.

Further, you will discover that possessing a "strong" ball will help you to cover such difficult spares as the 1–2–8, the 2–4–5–8, or the 1–3–9, where the ball must carry through to the back pin in order to make the spare.

THE PHYSIOLOGY OF BOWLING

I should like to call your attention to what I term the "Tensed Outer Muscle Theory of Bowling." Briefly, it means that when the *outside* muscles of the arm and fingers are in tension, and therefore in control of the bowling delivery, there will be a lessened tendency toward wrist-turning or finger rotation, which will cause a wrongly thrown ball by "topping" or "over-turning." There can only be the proper "lift" forward to give the ball the correct start after the "squeeze" of the fingers.

Throughout the pendulum action of the bowling arc, backward and forward through the moment of delivery, the outer muscles of the arm and hand remain tense and are kept under constant tension. The elbow, acting as a hinge, is broken directly upward in a plane perpendicular to the floor at the moment of delivery. From start to finish, the entire shoulder and arm proceed backward and forward without any rotation or turning clockwise or counter-clockwise away from the beginning hand and arm position.

Now, I'd like you to prove something to yourself. Reach out in front of your body with your right hand and feel the tension in the outer muscles of your arm. Technically, these are the extensors. Then, with your arm extended, close your fist tightly and you will feel the inner muscles of your arm become activated. These are the flexors. Then, open your fist so that only the last three fingers are clenched. You will find that your thumb and first finger are controlled by different flexor muscles than the other three, and you have proof that the thumb and forefinger can be relaxed and yet you may have the clenched action of the SQUEEZE delivery.

Here is another interesting experiment for you to carry out in the "physiology of bowling." With your left hand clasped tightly just above your right wrist, attempt to turn your right wrist counterclockwise by using the right *wrist* alone. You cannot do it! Much of the ability to turn the wrist and consequently the fingers, too, arises in a turning movement which begins in the elbow socket. The rest arises in the shoulder and is accomplished by the elbow leaving the side of the body. All of which, in my opinion, merely gives strong physiological basis for the analysis that "the elbow, acting as a hinge, is broken directly upward in a plane perpendicular to the floor," and also further substantiates the necessity for "squareness to the line," or keeping the elbow tight to the right side and not allowing it to stray out from the body and thus permit unwanted wrist or finger rotation at the moment of delivery.

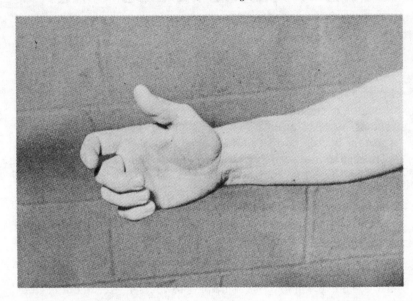

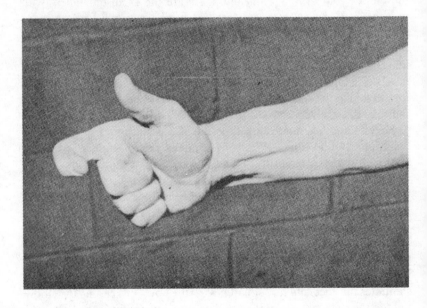

A Physical Proof of the Necessity for Leaning Forward

Here's another physical exercise I should like you to try: Stand up straight, as if you are facing an imaginary foul line, and draw your right arm back in an imaginary swing. Notice that at about a 30- to 35-degree angle you begin to feel a distinct binding sensation in your shoulder muscles and are soon prevented from any further backswing.

Now, lean forward from the waist and discover that the shoulder muscles no longer bind, that you are now enabled to complete a backswing to shoulder height without any difficulty. The obvious conclusion is that you must lean forward to accomplish a satisfactory backswing.

THE SECOND BALL

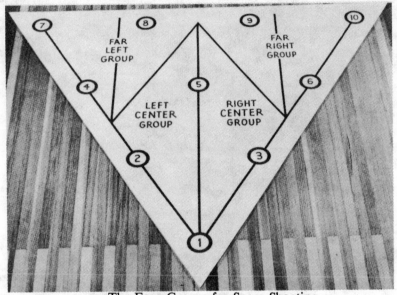

The Four Groups for Spare Shooting

This is a simple diagram of the various groupings which control your starting position in order to convert spares and many splits. You should memorize it! The 4–7–8 constitutes the Far Left Group, the 6–9–10, the Far Right Group. Reverse the name of the group and, in general, you have your starting position. Far Left—Far Right Starting Position, and vice versa. In the center of the alley is the Left Center Group which has the 1–2–5–8 pins and the Right Center Group with the 1–3–5–9 pins. You will see in a moment how the presence or absence of the 5 pin makes quite a difference in your starting position to convert the Center Group spares. Left Center Group spares, in general, are bowled from Right Center Starting Position and Right Center Group spares from Left Center Starting Position.

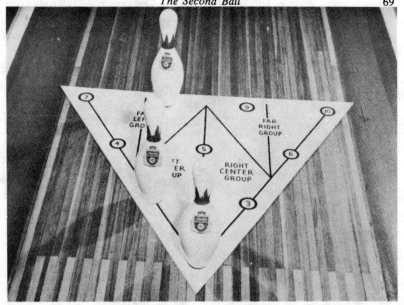

The Left Center Group (without the 5 Pin)

The 1–2–8 group constitutes the Left Center Group (without the 5 pin) and should be bowled from Strike Position, "Brooklyn Hit." By this expression, I mean that you start from your normal strike position with your left toe on the center spot but by picking out one board left of your strike board or strike "line" at the "break of the boards," which you can see in the following picture, your ball will travel across the alley into the 1–2 pocket and will take the 8 pin out on its way through. The addition of the 4 or 7 pin makes no difference to this setup. Always bowl from Strike Position, "Brooklyn Hit."

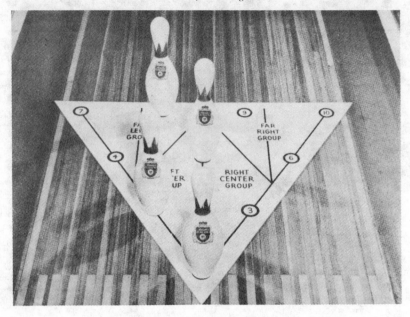

The Left Center Group (with the 5 Pin)

The 1–2–5–8 constitutes the Left Center Group and is bowled from Strike Position over your normal "strike" line right into the 1–3 "pocket." This cluster might just as well be an entire setup of ten pins. The 5 pin is the controlling factor here and the ball must be thrown with "action," that is, with the proper finger "squeeze" so that the 5 pin is taken out. If you should happen to have either the 4 pin or the 7 pin or both added to the Left Center Group you will still bowl from the Strike Position, inasmuch as the Center Group's importance and position control your decision.

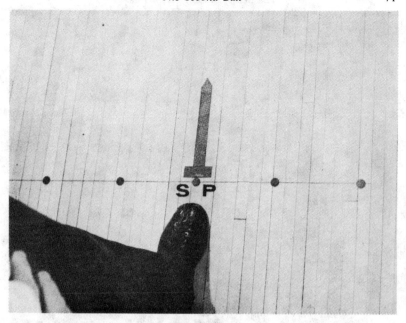

Strike Position·

As you will remember, your starting position for a strike hit in the 1–3 pocket found your left foot on the center dot and your right shoulder in line with your "strike line" or "board" or "spot." For the Left Center Group (with the 5 pin) you will always bowl from your natural Strike Position primarily because of the presence of the 5 pin. Since it is the "kingpin" and hard to get out of the cluster, your strike "angle" is the best one to use.

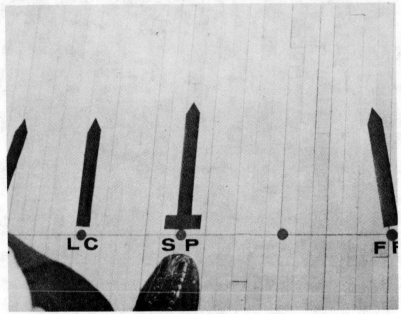

Strike Position, "Brooklyn Hit"

Notice that you are still in your normal strike starting position with your left foot on the center dot. But this time, by aiming one board left of your normal strike "spot" at the "break of the boards," your ball will travel from six to eight inches left of your usual "strike" line. The result is that it will come in on the 1–2 or "Brooklyn" pocket in very much the same manner that it would have come into the 1–3 pocket if you had not aimed the single board left.

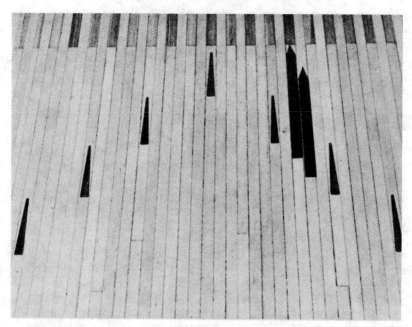

Choosing Your Board or "Line" for "Strike Position, Brooklyn Hit"

Notice the two black arrows that have been applied to the alley between the second and third "diamond" indicators from the right. The arrow on the right represents your normal "spot," board, or line which takes your ball into the 1–3 "strike pocket." The arrow on the board to its left shows the line that the ball must travel in order to "cross over" the headpin and hit the 1–2 pocket for a "Brooklyn Hit." You do not change your starting position. You merely run one board left of your usual strike position line and the slight resulting "angle" does the work of bringing the ball into the 1–2 pocket.

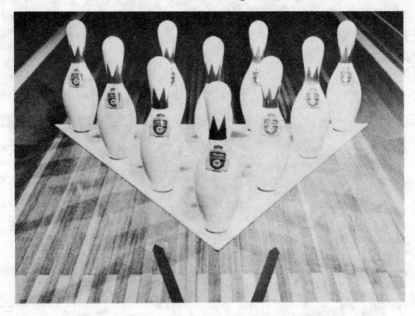

Far Left and Far Right Bowling "Angle"

The two black arrows you see in the foreground of the picture above indicate the "cross alley" angle, which results from your starting from Far Right Starting Position and Far Left Starting Position. It is this "angling for your spares" which takes advantage of the width of the ball track to help you knock down the greatest number of pins.

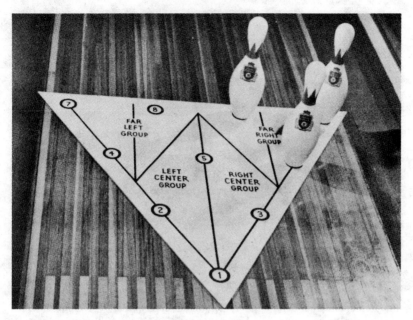

The Far Right Group

The 6, the 9 and the 10 pins are in the Far Right Group and you should always bowl for them from Far Left Starting Position. The only exception to this suggestion is that you may find that you can make the 9 pin alone from the Left Center Position since it is also a part of that group. But if you have the 6 pin standing with either the 9 pin or the 10 pin you have a better "angle," and therefore a better chance to convert, by rolling from the Far Left Starting Position.

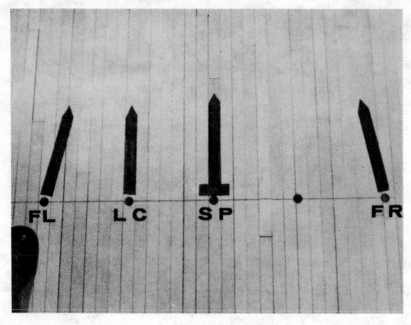

Far Left Starting Position

Place your left foot on the fourteenth dot left of your center or "strike" dot. Face directly toward the pins on the far right side of the lane. Your approach will be directly toward the pins and definitely "cross alley." However, you must be aware of the fact that, since your ball will be delivered from the right-hand side of your body, your actual delivery point at the foul line will be at about the middle of the alley. Swing your arm directly toward the pins and do not "ease up" in any manner. Use Far Left Starting Position for Far Right Group spares.

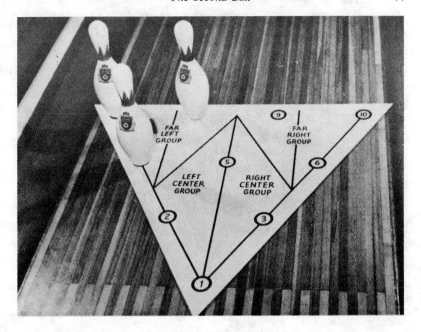

The Far Left Group

The 4, the 7 and the 8 pins are in the Far Left Group and should almost without exception be bowled from Far Right Starting Position. Always remember to allow for the extra distance the ball must travel to get into the third or the back row of pins, and choose a "line" or "spot" slightly to the right of the line your eye tells you to use. You will find that most spares are missed on the left-hand side because of the failure to make this suggested allowance.

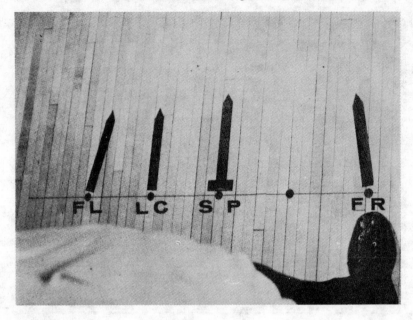

Far Right Starting Position

Place your left foot on the fourteenth dot to the right of the center dot and square yourself directly toward the pins in the Far Left Group. If the 8 pin is standing alone, you may prefer to bowl from Strike Position, "Brooklyn Hit," but in general if you have the 4 pin alone, the 7 pin alone, or both 4 pin and 7 pin, you are better off to use the entire width of the alley in "angling" for your spare. You will miss less often, if you do.

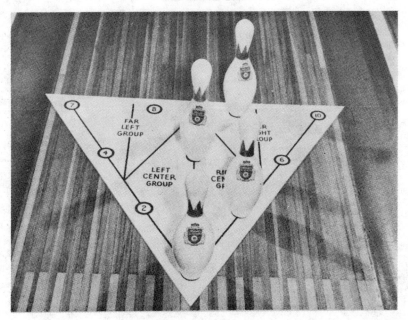

The Right Center Group

The 1, 3, 5 and 9 pins constitute the Right Center Group and you will use Left Center Starting Position to convert these pins or nearly any combination of them. If you have pins added from the Far Right Group such as the 6 or the 10 or perhaps both of them, your best strategy is to remain in the Left Center Starting Position in order to decrease your chances of cutting off one or more pins. If the 5 pin is present, experiment to find whether for you it is easier to convert the Right Center Group spares from Strike Position or from Left Center. But, once you find it out, stay with it from then on. Don't vary.

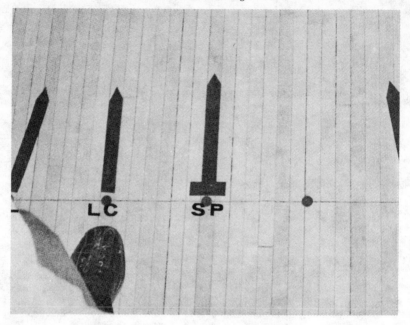

Left Center Starting Position

Place your left foot on the seventh dot left of the center dot and square yourself toward the pins and your spare, just as if you are throwing a first ball. You will be delivering this ball slightly across the alley. This starting position is used for Right Center Group pins. If your spare has pins in both Right Center Group and Far Right Group, the importance of getting the Center Group pins determines your starting position and controls your start from Left Center.

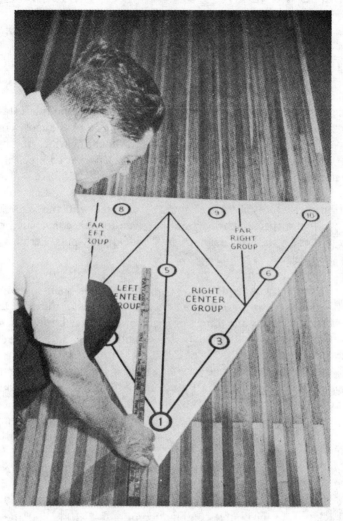

Why It Is So Easy to Miss a "Sleeper" Pin

It is 22½ inches from the head pin to the 5 pin and also from the 3 back to the 9 or from the 2 to the 8. When you realize that the other pins such as the 3, the 5 and the 6 are only one foot apart, and when you study the illustration, you can see why it is easy for the ball to be deflected off the front pin and miss the rear pin. "Tandems" such as the 3–9 combination or the 2–8 are tough to convert. Practice hitting them head-on with power to carry through the long distance to the back pin.

SPLITS AND WHAT TO DO ABOUT THEM

A split is a leave of two or more pins with the head pin down and a gap of at least one pin between any other two pins.

You have a "split" when two or more pins are left standing after a first ball and the space of a missing pin or pins remains between them, making it more difficult to "convert" or "make the split." Technically, under American Bowling Congress rules, if the head pin is left standing no "split" is designated, but, in my opinion, one of the most colorful conversions ever made is the 1–2–10 "washout" in which the bowler rolls his second ball into the left-hand (1–2) pocket so precisely that the number 1 pin is sharply driven across the alley to take out the 10 pin. Since the head pin, number 1, happened to be standing, this conversion merits only a "spare" mark. I disagree with the A.B.C. and believe that a special mark should be given for this conversion, or for that matter for the conversion of any "wide-open" splits. Perhaps some day the rule will be changed.

For, as you will find out by experience, or you already know, there are moderately wide and "wide-open" splits. Wide-open splits are always those with two pins or more on opposite sides of the alley and in the same row, either the third row together or the back row. These are so difficult to convert that they are usually called "impossible." But once in a long while the A.B.C. will award a special arm patch for the bowling shirt of anyone who has been accurate enough, or lucky enough, to convert the "Big Four," the 4–6–7–10 split, or you will hear of someone making the 4–6, the 8–10, or the 7–9. Sometimes this happens when one pin is hit so hard that it flies up into the rack or into the padding at the back of the pit and ricochets back into the alley to clear the other pin.

Splits can be classified into three types namely, the "impossible," the "fit-it-in-between," and the "slide-it-over" splits.

If you have left the 4–6 split in the third row, the 8–10, or the 7–9 in the back row, or the double combination of 4–6–7–10 in both the third row and back row, you have one of the "impossibles." Let's consider these "impossible" splits and decide what to do about them when they occur.

First, why are these considered "impossible"? Because, since two of the pins left are on the same line with each other, no matter what angle the ball strikes one of the pins, it is practically impossible to drive it over at an angle acute enough to take out the other pin. Now, rarely this does happen; and once in a great while, as we mentioned, one pin will fly back into the kickbacks and rebound onto the alley to take out the remaining pin in the split. However, it is better not to plan on these unlikely occurrences. Try to knock down at least one of these pins, and if you get the 4–6–7–10, try to knock down two or even three of the pins. You will see how to get three pins in our discussion of the "slide-it-over" splits.

These are splits which are apparently "wide-open" at first glance and impossible but are, in actuality, possible because one pin is in the row in front of the other or others and can be made by bowling at the front pin in such a way as to slide it over against the other pins and thus "convert" or "make the split."

The "fit-it-in-between" splits, as the name implies, are those that can be made by bowling at the space between the pins, striking one to the right and the other to the left.

Study the following diagrams and pictures and learn to recognize the splits which are "impossible" and those which can be made with skill (and luck!) and your bowling enjoyment will increase immeasurably.

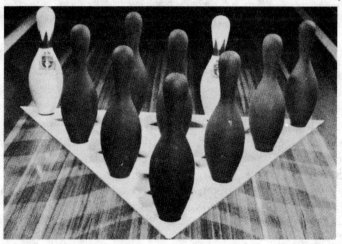

The 7–9 "Impossible" Split

Make sure that you knock down at least one of these pins. If you are bowling in practice, always practice on your hardest pin. If you have been missing the 7 pin, practice on it. Try moving one board left or right from your normal "Far Right" starting position just to see what effect the moves have on the ball action. Or you might try the same from "Left Center" position on the 9 pin. In league play don't experiment, get your easiest pin and the greatest "count" possible.

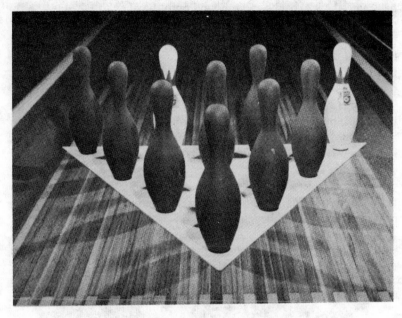

The 8–10 "Impossible" Split

This split usually occurs when your ball "dies" or "flattens" on a pocket 1–3 hit. It is a nasty split and a discouraging one because you have had hopes that you might get a strike. Don't lose the opportunity to practice on the 10 pin, that is, if you are bowling in practice. You might even practice on the 3–10 split by imagining the 3 pin in front of the 10. If you are in competition, count your easiest pin, whichever one it is. Bowl for the 8 from Strike Position, "Brooklyn Hit."

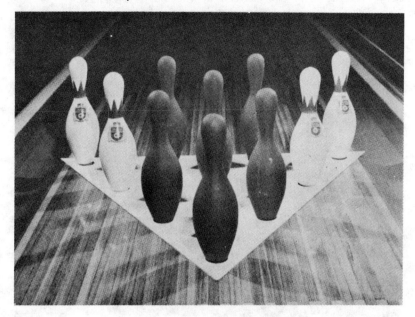

The 4–6–7–10 "Impossible" Split

This split pops up when your ball goes in directly on the "nose" or head pin and usually without much action. It is a dread split and fortunately quite infrequent. Take advantage of its scoring possibilities and count as many pins as you can. From your experience, you will know whether you convert the 4–7–10 or the 6–7–10 split more often and so pretend that you have either one of those. Forget about the fourth pin up and by converting the 4–7–10 or 6–7–10 out of this combination, you might get lucky and spill either the 7 or 10 pin forward to make the entire split. If you do, A.B.C. will reward you with a special arm patch, the occurrence is so rare!

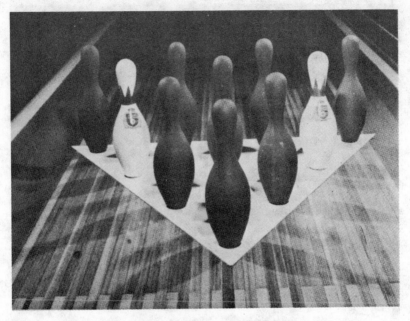

The 4–6 "Impossible" Split

This split, like the 4–6–7–10, happens when your ball hits too high on the head pin. In competition, bowl at your easiest pin and be sure to convert it. In practice, bowl at your hardest pin and try to hit the difficult pin in a particular spot, its left side, its right side, or exactly in the middle. Or you might practice on an imaginary 4–7–10 or 6–7–10 split and try to clip the 4 or the 6 pin thin enough to slide over and take out the imaginary 7 or 10 pin. If you do it, it is as much fun as making it in reality.

The "Fit-it-in-between" Splits

From our discussion on "Taking Advantage of the 'Angle' " and from the picture above, you can see that you have about 2 inches more in ball width than the distance between the two pins, the 5–6, the 4–5, the 7–8 or 9–10. So, these splits, along with the two "baby" splits—the 3–10 and the 2–7—are possible to convert by fitting the ball between the pins, hitting each pin and knocking them both down. Remember your "angles" and you can convert these splits regularly. And they're fun to make!

The 5–6 "Fit-it-in-between" Split

Bowl this split from Left Center Position. It usually results from a "cross-over" type of hit, going away from the head pin on the left. It is a harder split than the similar 4–5 split because you have to move from your normal starting position and because your ball will be traveling a line not frequently used and consequently of unknown characteristics. Be sure to allow a little more to the right than your eye tells you, as the pins are in the third row and your ball will be "taking off" in its curve in the last foot or so of its travel.

The 3–10 "Fit-it-in-between" Split

Bowl from Far Left Position. There are several different mental approaches to this split. Some bowlers shoot for the 10 pin and trust that the curve of the ball will bring it in on the right side of the 3 pin and that the deflection of the ball will take out the 10 pin. Another trick is to imagine the missing 6 pin and shoot to hit it dead on. Still another method is to roll the ball either directly for, or slightly to the left of, the particular spot at the "break of the boards," which results in a 10-pin conversion for you. Experiment with all these methods and find the best way for you.

The 4–5 "Fit-it-in-between" Split

Start in Strike Position, "Brooklyn Hit," and you can fit your ball between these two pins. From my observation, this split is usually missed on the left because the bowler forgets that the pins are farther away in the third row, 22 inches beyond the head pin. So be sure to over-allow to the right and you may have a better chance to make the split. Another trick is to imagine the missing 8 pin and shoot for it, forgetting about the two in front of it. Sometimes this works because it is relaxing to think of a spare rather than a split.

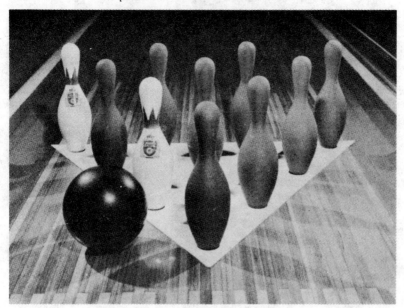

The 2–7 "Fit-it-in-between" Split

Bowl from Far Right Position. You can either shoot for the "ghost" 4 pin between the 2 and the 7 or for the left side of the 2 pin, but you will find that this "baby split" can be converted quite often. It is easier than the opposite 3–10 because your ball will be curving in toward the 7 pin and helping you to make it. Practice on this split and on the right-hand 3–10 "baby split" and you should convert them with regularity.

Why It Is So Easy to Be "Tapped" on a 10 Pin, a 7 Pin, or a 4 Pin

Sometimes your strike ball seems to get under all the pins and starts them revolving in a horizontal plane and all the pins go down. And then again, sometimes your ball seems to knock the pins straight across the alley. Always remember that you may have a lovely 15-inch-wide track clearing out pins for you if your pins fly crossways, but if they go straight through you have only a 4-inch track. That's why you will often lose a pin or two on what seems to be a good hit! Don't worry about it; the luck evens out.

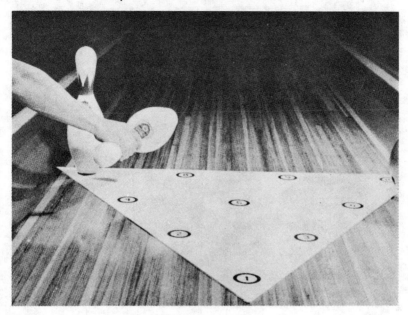

The "Slide-it-over" Splits

As you can see from the illustration above and from the photographs that follow, if one of the pins is in the line in front of the others even though the split is "wide open," it is not only possible but entirely practicable to convert this type of split. This is done by striking the pin in the front line at the proper angle so as to clip it over across the alley to take out the remaining pin. Your practice on the 10 pin and on the 4 and 6 pins will help you to make the "slide-it-over" splits often—and there is no greater thrill in bowling, let me assure you!

The 4–7–10 "Slide-it-over" Split

Bowl this split from Far Right Position. Plan to clip the 4 pin on its left side so as to slide it over and take out the 10 pin. The 4 pin must be hit extremely "thin." This split is much more difficult to make than the reverse split the 6–7–10 because your ball is "going away" from the 4 pin. I believe in aiming for the 7 pin and forgetting about the 4 pin if I am trying to make this split. In league competition, don't try to make it unless it is urgently needed. Get the two pins on the left side and take advantage of your "count."

The 4–7–9 "Slide-it-over" Split

This split occurs on a "high" hit on the head pin and indicates that you should adjust your "angle" to come in more toward the 3 pin. Roll from Far Right Position and aim at the 7 pin alone. Shave the 4 pin on its left-hand side and you will clip it over to take out the 9 pin. This split is easier to make than the 4–7–10 because the 9 pin is a foot closer than the 10 pin. Sometimes it helps to pretend that you don't have the 9 pin standing and bowl for a thin 4–7 conversion. You can make it!

The 5–10 "Slide-it-over" Split

This split is like the 8–10 split, an indicator of a weak ball, one that has failed to get in to the 5 pin, has "flattened" and "died" in the pocket. If you get this split or the 8–10 quite often, you are not using the proper finger action. Get back to fundamentals, roll the ball, making sure your thumb is out first and that you are "squeezing" at the delivery point. Make the 5–10 from Strike Position, "Brooklyn Hit." If you find it hard to make from this position, try moving a little left. It may work better for you. Experiment. Find your best "angle" and then stay with it until you are forced to change.

The 5–7 "Slide-it-over" Split

There is a trick to making this split and once you learn it, you will find that you are converting it often. If you will remember, bowling from Strike Position to the board or left of your normal strike line brings you into the 1–2 pocket and results in what we call Strike Position, "Brooklyn Hit." If you will move just one board left of your strike starting position with your left foot, and throw your ball over your strike line or strike "spot" at the "break of the boards" your ball will be coming in sharply on the right-hand side of the 5 pin and you can snap it over smartly to take out the 7 pin. Practice hard on this and you can make it one out of three times!

The 6–7–10 "Slide-it-over" Split

Start from Far Left Position and shoot directly for the 10 pin. Try to hit the 10 pin on its right side, even to the extent of missing the 6 pin. The result will be that your ball will be "coming in" strongly on the right-hand side of the 6 pin and will snap it over sharply to take out the 7 pin. Use good speed on this conversion and you have a better chance to make it. A slow ball or one that just touches the 6 pin often slides it over either in front of the 7 pin or so slowly that it will not knock it down. That is most discouraging.

OTHER VARIATIONS IN CONVERTING SPARES

The 1–2–8 Spare, Left Center Group

This spare, the 1–2, the 1–2–4–8, the 1–2–4–7 and the delightful 1–2–10 "washout" are all bowled in exactly the same manner, from Strike Position, "Brooklyn Hit." Since you are in your familiar starting position you should be more relaxed than usual. It is not hard to hit that board to the left of your strike line, and if you do you will carry through to take out the 8 pin with your strong ball. Don't fail to give your ball the "squeeze," for you must have as much "action" on this or the other named spares as you need on your first ball to strike.

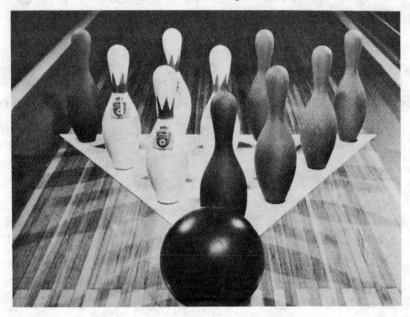

The 2–4–5–8 Spare, Left Center Group

Bowl this spare from Right Center Starting Position. Pretend that you have a "baby strike" setup and plan to hit firmly in the 2–5 pocket. You have to rely on the 2 pin taking out the 4 pin and so your hit has to be high on the 2 pin. This is a hateful spare and a much dreaded one. Be sure to concentrate on your finger action because your ball must have "stuff" on it to help it get through to the 8 pin. If you miss your pocket and come in on the left side, you may still be lucky enough to convert it by having the 2 pin get the 5 and the ball take the 8 away. Practice on this spare a great deal and you will lose your fear of it.

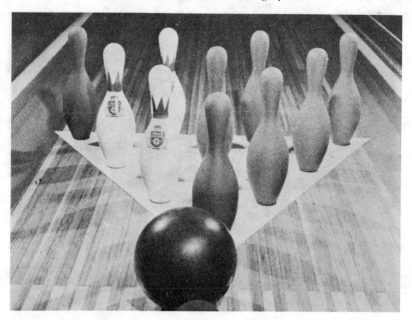

The 2–4–8 Spare, Left Center Group

This spare is a blood brother to the nasty 2–4–5–8 spare just discussed. It is a little easier because the 5 pin is gone, but don't fail to work hard on converting it. Bowl from Strike Position, "Brooklyn Hit," and come in high on the 2 pin so as to deflect it into the 4 pin, and be sure that the ball has the "action" to carry through to take out the 8 pin. You can't make this spare very often if you hit in the 2–4 pocket because the ball will deflect away from the 8 pin and leave it standing. Another one of those spares it is better not to leave!

The 2-Pin Spare, Left Center Group

You should be able to bowl this spare with your eyes closed. You have practiced and practiced on your Strike Position start, which brings your ball into the 1–3 pocket and on your Strike Position, "Brooklyn Hit," which brings your ball into the 1–2 pocket. Remember that you have a target area of 23 inches to hit and be sure that you hit it. Use this single pin for practice on your 1–2 pocket hit and for making the imaginary 1–2–10 "washout." Picture the 8 pin back of it and work on making that "tandem" or "sleeper" leave. Watch where the ball goes to make sure it would have taken out the imaginary 8 pin!

The 2–8 Spare, Left Center Group

Now that you have been practicing on the 1–2 pocket from Strike Position, "Brooklyn Hit," you have the opportunity to prove that you can hit it with authority. The 2 pin must be hit on the right-hand side and the ball must have enough power of its own to overcome the tendency to deflect away from the 8 pin. The ball will take out the 8 pin. Sometimes you may miss your target and still get the break of having the 2 pin fly back to take out the 8 pin. Don't count on it! The distance is the same 22 inches that the 5 pin is away from the head pin, and your chances that it will happen are remote.

The 1–2–4–7 Spare, Left Center Group

Bowl this "clothesline" or "fence post" from Strike Position, "Brooklyn Hit." Any time you leave more than one pin in a spare you are in danger of missing. So here your danger is quadrupled. You must have the help of the 4 pin to take out the 7 after your ball has hit into the "Brooklyn" 1–2 pocket. Your ball must have "action" in order to deflect as far as the 4 pin, so be certain that you apply the "squeeze." If you move too far right to make this spare you will find that you may miss the head pin. Any way you shoot for it, it is a very difficult spare and quite a pleasure to convert.

The 1–2–10 "Washout" Spare

Bowl this from Strike Position, "Brooklyn Hit" and you can convert this troublesome spare without too much difficulty. It usually results from a ball that is thrown out too far on the alley and consequently begins to act too late and "gets behind" the head pin. It also indicates a "flat ball" or one without proper finger action. On your spare be sure that you keep your thumb to the left and that you accomplish the "squeeze" and the head pin will be snapped over and across the alley to take out the 10.

The 2–5 Spare, Left Center Group

This is an exception to the rule on groupings. For the reason that the curving ball is apt to cut off the front pin of these two, most good bowlers move to their left and shoot at this spare from either head-on or even slightly left of head-on in order to cut down the "chop" angle and make the ball track take care of the back pin. Try all the positions on this spare, and once you find one that helps you to cover them regularly, stay with it. Try bowling at the 5 pin alone, or at the 2 pin alone, and forgetting that the other is up. It may help.

The 2–4–5 Spare, Left Center Group

This spare results from a very thin hit on the right hand side of the head pin. Since there are three pins, it is a difficult spare and it is easy to "pick" either the 4 pin or the 5 pin. The best way to make it is to bowl from Strike Position, "Brooklyn Hit," so as to come into the 2–5 pocket strongly enough to cause the 2 pin to go back into the 4 and take it out while the ball takes the 5. This strategy is good, too, in case you "pull" your ball left, which you might do, for then you may still hit in the 2–4 pocket and still get the 5 pin with the 2 pin. The best advice on this spare is "Don't leave it!"

The 4–7 Spare, Far Left Group

This spare is so easy that you have to be careful about it. Bowl from Far Right Position and don't forget to use the "squeeze." If your ball flattens—and it is possible for it has to travel 3 feet or so farther—it might catch the 4 pin on its right side so thin that the 4 pin "wraps around" the 7. You should never miss this spare on the left-hand side. If you do, it indicates that you have loafed and lost your speed. If you want to, practice on the imaginary 4–7–10 split and slide the 4 over to take out the imaginary 10 pin. In league play, however, don't experiment. Get your two-pin count every time.

The 2–4–7 Spare, Far Left Group

Bowl this spare from Far Right Starting Position. Plan to hit the 2 pin on its left side and the ball will deflect into the 4 and possibly all the way to the 7. If not, the 4 pin will take the 7 pin out. If you come in too directly on the 4 pin you may hit it too far on its right side and "wrap it around" the 7 pin. This spare is not too difficult because your ball will be curving into the pins. Once in a while it is made "on the outside" by striking the 2 pin on its right side and letting the pins take each other out. It is not the safe way to do it although you may get away with it.

The 7-Pin Spare, Far Left Group

Bowl from Far Right Starting Position. Although this pin is like the 10 pin in having a smaller target than usual because it is so close to the gutter, it is not as hard a pin to knock down as the 10 pin, because your ball is curving into it rather than away from it. Don't ever "loaf" on a 7 or 10 pin, or you will find yourself missing the pin on the left. Sometimes, too, by loafing you may forget to give your ball the "squeeze" and it may die short of the pin and miss on the right. Be careful, line yourself up facing the pin, and walk directly toward the 7 pin. Try to hit it squarely, or at least on the right side, and you won't miss it very often.

The 3–6–9 Spare, Right Center Group

It is very easy to "pick a cherry" on this spare, so be careful not to move too far left, for if you do your ball may take out the 3 and 6 pins and leave the 9 pin standing. By bowling from Left Center, your ball can come in high and hard on the 3 and 9, and the 3 will either go back and take out the 9 while the ball takes the 6 pin, or the ball will knock the 3 pin to its left and go through and take out both 6 and 9 pins. Practice on this spare so you can cover the 3 and 9 and you will rarely leave the 6 standing.

The 1–3–6–10 Spare, Right Center Group

The fact that you have the 1 and 3 pins in this wicked leave controls your strategy as to whether to bowl this from Far Left or Left Center. Your ball must hit in the 1–3 pocket and get some help from the 6 pin in taking out the 10 pin. If you move too far left in an attempt to "cover" them all you will probably slide by the head pin. Once in a while this can be made "on the outside," clipping the head pin on its left side, but your probabilities are much more remote than they are by using the ball to do some of the work. It's a hard spare, especially for a strong curve ball which is breaking away from the pins. Don't be too upset if you miss it.

The 6–10 Spare, Far Right Group

This spare, along with the 5–9 and the 2–5 spares, is difficult for the right-hand bowler with a strong "hook" because of the tendency of the hook to cut sharply through the front pin and cut it off from the pin to the right. You may find that you can lessen the number of your "chops" by aiming for the pin to the right and trying to hit it full, using as much angle as you can. The more angle, the less the chance for the "cherry pick," in general. Roll for the 6–10 from Far Left Starting Position. Your ball will usually "come up" the inch or so necessary to take out the front pin.

The 5–9 Spare, Right Center Group

This leave very often happens on a "Brooklyn" or 1–2 pocket hit where the ball is going away too radically to the left of the head pin. It is a hard spare because of the chance to "pick a cherry" out of either pin. By bowling from Left Center Starting Position you will have the best "angle" to make this spare. Be sure to roll the ball a little faster because the pins are farther back than usual and if you start sliding by the 5 pin and taking the 9 out on the right side, move a little to your right until you find that you are getting the 5 and leaving the 9. Everybody "chops" this once in a while, so don't worry too much if you do, too!

The 6–9–10 Spare, Far Right Group

Start in Far Left Position. Play this as a "baby" strike so as to hit in the right-hand pocket. Forget about the 9 pin as you will probably get it with the 6 pin while the ball takes out the 10 pin. If you "pull" your ball a little left, or if it runs farther than you thought it would, you may still make the spare "on the outside," but it isn't the best way to do it.

The 10–Pin Spare, Far Right Group

Start in Far Left Position. Because this pin is in the back row and because of the tendency of your ball to "run" left at the last moment, you must throw harder and faster at the 10 pin to cover it. Be sure that you square your body to the pin and walk directly toward it. You must follow through on this pin especially, because if you "loaf" you will be sure to pull your ball left and miss. Some bowlers imagine a pin standing in the gutter to the right and aim for it. Always try to hit the 10 pin flush and it will help you to convert the 6–10 spare when you have it.

Why It Is So Easy to Miss the 10 Pin

Notice that because the 10 pin is only 2½ inches from the right-hand gutter, you do not get the advantage of the entire ball width on the right side. The same thing holds true, in reverse, for the 7 pin on its left side. Since your target is some seven inches narrower than on other one-pin spares, be especially careful and take advantage of the "angle" and get the 10 pin or the 7 pin on its "good" side!

HOW TO THROW A STRAIGHT BALL

It is possible that this book has not achieved its purpose of making it so clear and simple that it is easy to throw a strike ball with "action" imparted by the easily learned "squeeze." And so, most regretfully, I will show you how to throw a ball without the "squeeze" and tell you that when you do you will be throwing a straight ball. All you have to do is let your thumb be pointed directly at the head pin and let the ball come off your fingers without any wrist turn or movement whatsoever, and without any "squeeze action" of the fingers. You will, of necessity, move several boards to your right and direct the ball straight into the 1–3 pocket. All the other advice I have given you on spares or splits you will correct by moving to compensate for the lack of curve on the last few feet of your ball track. Don't expect ever to be a good bowler. You may become a respectable bowler, perhaps average in the 150's, but your ball will be subject to such deflection that you will have more splits than the average bowler who throws a ball with "the squeeze" and its consequent "action."

Front View of the Delivery of a Straight Ball

All the fundamentals of the bowling delivery apply for the straight ball. The body remains "square to the line," but since the line for a straight ball is from the corner of the alley from Right Center Position or even from Far Right Position, the squareness of the hips and body is toward a line directly into the 1–3 pocket. You will find it very difficult to throw a true "straight" ball. The wrist at the last second will give a slight turn one way or the other and the ball will either curve slightly left or "back up" right. Either way, you will find that it is difficult to knock down a great many pins because of the deflection of the ball.

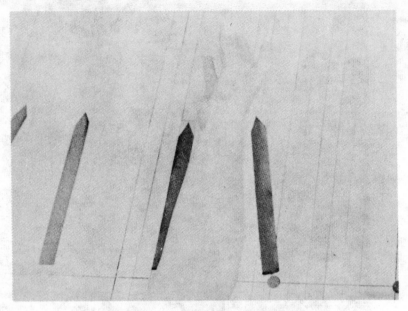

The Hand Action for the Straight Ball

Bowl the straight ball from the right-hand side of the approach and slant directly in toward the head pin and the 1–3 pocket. Adjust your starting position according to the suggestions earlier in this book, moving "with your error." All the other fundamentals of bowling apply just as well to the straight ball, the squareness to the line, the timing, the relaxation, the firm wrist. Just don't squeeze!

SOME COMMON FAULTS IN BOWLING

Here is a demonstration of one of the major faults which the bowler must avoid. This fault is called "side-wheeling" and, just as the name implies, is caused by the bowler turning his body away from the necessary squareness to the line. By turning clockwise the ball is caused to come around behind the bowler's body and at the delivery moment is thrown with the elbow out, away from the bowler's side, causing an "overturning" action, the fingers being on top of the ball and physically in no position to apply the squeeze. The ball comes off the thumb and has no action on the pins. Usually this type of hand action causes a sore thumb, as all the weight of the ball is thrown against the thumb instead of being carried in the fingers, and the spin off the thumb wears the skin rather severely.

Here is another major fault the bowler must avoid. It is the opposite of side-wheeling and is caused by taking the ball in the backswing in a definite "outside" arc. The result is that the elbow strays from its proper position tight to the bowler's side, and in the downswing the ball is caused to roll on a line crossing inward to the left of the head pin. Although sometimes action may be imparted to the ball by the fingers at the explosion point, usually a bad hit results on the left of the head pin and a split is apt to occur. Quite often, too, this type of fault results in a "topped" action at the delivery point where the fingers are ahead of their proper position and consequently in no position to work properly in their squeezing action. Most important is the fact that with this fault the bowler cannot roll down his proper line.

Here is a third major fault exemplified in this mock delivery, namely, letting the hand and ball get out away from the body at the explosion point. This is usually caused by the failure of the bowler to maintain his straight approach. He "slants" in toward the center of the alley, and, realizing that he has slanted in, he makes either one or the other of two mistakes. If he maintains his approach to the left, he throws his ball to the left and not on his intended line. Secondly, if he realizes that he has slanted in and still wants to throw down his line, he must let his arm wander out from his body in the position away from the left foot at explosion point; from this angle little or no action can be imparted.

DEVELOP YOUR OWN STYLE

About starting positions—you have been told rather definitely, "Put your left foot here or there on a particular spot!" Actually what this book has attempted to do is to give you a point of reference from which you can start to develop your own bowling game and style. Some people take longer steps than others and so it is entirely possible that your starting position should be from 6 inches to a foot or more in front of or even behind the particular "dot" I have discussed.

The best way for you to determine your starting position distance away from the foul line is to reverse your approach. Start at the foul line and walk away from the foul line in what would be your normal walking steps. Then, add a half step for your slide and you will have your starting position within a few inches.

Don't be afraid to change your starting position closer or farther away from the foul line as you go along and your game develops. Sometimes shortening your footwork a few inches may make a world of difference in the compactness of your delivery. Or, lengthening it may put additional "steam" into your ball. Experiment!

After you have begun to standardize your bowling delivery and can count on 6 inches or more of "hook" at the end of your ball track, then you can depart moderately from the exact orders I have given in this book. But nearly all the starting positions I have set up for you remain consistently valid in relation to one another and in relation to the various angles which are recommended for the conversion of the spares or splits. However, if you find that you can convert the 10 pin, or for that matter any other pin or spare, by going completely contrary to the recommended "angle" (that is, by bowling for the 10 pin from Far Right Position, as an example), by all means bowl for that spare from the angle you have found. The purpose of this game is to knock down the most pins, convert the most spares and splits, and thereby get the highest total score.

In my own case, I find it difficult to get as far left as I suggest to you. It is not that I don't want to do it. It merely happens that one of the lanes I bowl on has a wall close to its left-hand end alley, and I find that if I take all the room I want on the other alleys when I have the room available, in bowling on the end alley I am cramped and consequently rather upset at the forced change in my delivery on right-hand spares. Another thing that affects my bowling is that my right foot swings around behind me at the moment of delivery and sometimes I hit the ball-return rack with my ankle. I have to be careful not to get too far left as a result, and perhaps you may find the same conditions affecting your bowling.

Some people find it constitutionally impossible to walk a straight line. If you find that you cannot do so, it may be that the starting positions I have suggested for the straight-line walker are all wrong for you. Again I say, "Experiment." Understand the theory and put it into practice, adapting the various suggestions to fit your own individual case.

You may bowl in an old type of alley without the new "range-finders" or arrow-like markers to help you to find your "line" or "spot." This may be disconcerting for a while but really all you have to do is to take the time and effort to *count the various boards from the right-hand* gutter at the "break of the boards" and at your starting position and thereby find your starting spot and your line. Most old-fashioned lanes have a center peg in the center of the alley near the front of the approach. By using this center peg as a point of reference you can place your left foot either at that peg mark or a board or two one way or the other away from it. Also, you will find by close observation that every lane has varying colors of wood at the jagged "break of the boards" and that without too much difficulty you can pick out one board that is either lighter than the others or darker and thus determine your point of reference. Perhaps you will not bowl directly over that particular board, but you can say to yourself, "I'll try rolling one board inside that black board" and there will have your "line" or "spot."

I want to encourage you to become a better bowler. You can do it if you want to and I sincerely hope that this book will help you to achieve an enviable ambition, "to know what you are doing" when you bowl and thus have worlds more fun in bowling!

MELVIN POWERS SELF-IMPROVEMENT LIBRARY

ASTROLOGY

BRIDGE

BUSINESS, STUDY & REFERENCE

CALLIGRAPHY

CHESS & CHECKERS

___ SOVIET CHESS *Edited by R. G. Wade*		3.00

COOKERY & HERBS

___ CULPEPER'S HERBAL REMEDIES *Dr. Nicholas Culpeper*	3.00
___ FAST GOURMET COOKBOOK *Poppy Cannon*	2.50
___ GINSENG The Myth & The Truth *Joseph P. Hou*	3.00
___ HEALING POWER OF HERBS *May Bethel*	4.00
___ HEALING POWER OF NATURAL FOODS *May Bethel*	5.00
___ HERB HANDBOOK *Dawn MacLeod*	3.00
___ HERBS FOR HEALTH—How to Grow & Use Them *Louise Evans Doole*	4.00
___ HOME GARDEN COOKBOOK—Delicious Natural Food Recipes *Ken Kraft*	3.00
___ MEDICAL HERBALIST *edited by Dr. J. R. Yemm*	3.00
___ VEGETABLE GARDENING FOR BEGINNERS *Hugh Wiberg*	2.00
___ VEGETABLES FOR TODAY'S GARDENS *R. Milton Carleton*	2.00
___ VEGETARIAN COOKERY *Janet Walker*	7.00
___ VEGETARIAN COOKING MADE EASY & DELECTABLE *Veronica Vezza*	3.00
___ VEGETARIAN DELIGHTS—A Happy Cookbook for Health *K. R. Mehta*	2.00
___ VEGETARIAN GOURMET COOKBOOK *Joyce McKinnel*	3.00

GAMBLING & POKER

___ ADVANCED POKER STRATEGY & WINNING PLAY *A. D. Livingston*	5.00
___ HOW TO WIN AT DICE GAMES *Skip Frey*	3.00
___ HOW TO WIN AT POKER *Terence Reese & Anthony T. Watkins*	5.00
___ WINNING AT CRAPS *Dr. Lloyd T. Commins*	5.00
___ WINNING AT GIN *Chester Wander & Cy Rice*	3.00
___ WINNING AT POKER—An Expert's Guide *John Archer*	5.00
___ WINNING AT 21—An Expert's Guide *John Archer*	5.00
___ WINNING POKER SYSTEMS *Norman Zadeh*	3.00

HEALTH

___ BEE POLLEN *Lynda Lyngheim & Jack Scagnetti*	3.00
___ DR. LINDNER'S SPECIAL WEIGHT CONTROL METHOD *P. G. Lindner, M.D.*	2.00
___ HELP YOURSELF TO BETTER SIGHT *Margaret Darst Corbett*	3.00
___ HOW YOU CAN STOP SMOKING PERMANENTLY *Ernest Caldwell*	5.00
___ MIND OVER PLATTER *Peter G. Lindner, M.D.*	5.00
___ NATURE'S WAY TO NUTRITION & VIBRANT HEALTH *Robert J. Scrutton*	3.00
___ NEW CARBOHYDRATE DIET COUNTER *Patti Lopez-Pereira*	2.00
___ REFLEXOLOGY *Dr. Maybelle Segal*	4.00
___ REFLEXOLOGY FOR GOOD HEALTH *Anna Kaye & Don C. Matchan*	5.00
___ 30 DAYS TO BEAUTIFUL LEGS *Dr. Marc Selner*	3.00
___ YOU CAN LEARN TO RELAX *Dr. Samuel Gutwirth*	3.00
___ YOUR ALLERGY—What To Do About It *Allan Knight, M.D.*	3.00

HOBBIES

___ BEACHCOMBING FOR BEGINNERS *Norman Hickin*	2.00
___ BLACKSTONE'S MODERN CARD TRICKS *Harry Blackstone*	5.00
___ BLACKSTONE'S SECRETS OF MAGIC *Harry Blackstone*	5.00
___ COIN COLLECTING FOR BEGINNERS *Burton Hobson & Fred Reinfeld*	5.00
___ ENTERTAINING WITH ESP *Tony 'Doc' Shiels*	2.00
___ 400 FASCINATING MAGIC TRICKS YOU CAN DO *Howard Thurston*	5.00
___ HOW I TURN JUNK INTO FUN AND PROFIT *Sari*	3.00
___ HOW TO WRITE A HIT SONG & SELL IT *Tommy Boyce*	7.00
___ JUGGLING MADE EASY *Rudolf Dittrich*	3.00
___ MAGIC FOR ALL AGES *Walter Gibson*	4.00
___ MAGIC MADE EASY *Byron Wels*	2.00
___ STAMP COLLECTING FOR BEGINNERS *Burton Hobson*	3.00

HORSE PLAYERS' WINNING GUIDES

___ BETTING HORSES TO WIN *Les Conklin*	5.00
___ ELIMINATE THE LOSERS *Bob McKnight*	5.00
___ HOW TO PICK WINNING HORSES *Bob McKnight*	5.00
___ HOW TO WIN AT THE RACES *Sam (The Genius) Lewin*	5.00
___ HOW YOU CAN BEAT THE RACES *Jack Kavanagh*	5.00

_____ SEX WITHOUT GUILT *Albert Ellis, Ph.D.*		5.00
_____ SEXUALLY ADEQUATE MALE *Frank S. Caprio, M.D.*		3.00
_____ SEXUALLY FULFILLED MAN *Dr. Rachel Copelan*		5.00
_____ STAYING IN LOVE *Dr. Norton F. Kristy*		7.00

MELVIN POWERS' MAIL ORDER LIBRARY

_____ HOW TO GET RICH IN MAIL ORDER *Melvin Powers*		20.00
_____ HOW TO WRITE A GOOD ADVERTISEMENT *Victor O. Schwab*		20.00
_____ MAIL ORDER MADE EASY *J. Frank Brumbaugh*		20.00

METAPHYSICS & OCCULT

_____ BOOK OF TALISMANS, AMULETS & ZODIACAL GEMS *William Pavitt*		7.00
_____ CONCENTRATION—A Guide to Mental Mastery *Mouni Sadhu*		5.00
_____ EXTRA-TERRESTRIAL INTELLIGENCE—The First Encounter		6.00
_____ FORTUNE TELLING WITH CARDS *P. Foli*		5.00
_____ HOW TO INTERPRET DREAMS, OMENS & FORTUNE TELLING SIGNS *Gettings*		5.00
_____ HOW TO UNDERSTAND YOUR DREAMS *Geoffrey A. Dudley*		3.00
_____ ILLUSTRATED YOGA *William Zorn*		3.00
_____ IN DAYS OF GREAT PEACE *Mouni Sadhu*		3.00
_____ LSD—THE AGE OF MIND *Bernard Roseman*		2.00
_____ MAGICIAN—His Training and Work *W. E. Butler*		3.00
_____ MEDITATION *Mouni Sadhu*		7.00
_____ MODERN NUMEROLOGY *Morris C. Goodman*		5.00
_____ NUMEROLOGY—ITS FACTS AND SECRETS *Ariel Yvon Taylor*		5.00
_____ NUMEROLOGY MADE EASY *W. Mykian*		5.00
_____ PALMISTRY MADE EASY *Fred Gettings*		5.00
_____ PALMISTRY MADE PRACTICAL *Elizabeth Daniels Squire*		5.00
_____ PALMISTRY SECRETS REVEALED *Henry Frith*		4.00
_____ PROPHECY IN OUR TIME *Martin Ebon*		2.50
_____ SUPERSTITION—Are You Superstitious? *Eric Maple*		2.00
_____ TAROT *Mouni Sadhu*		10.00
_____ TAROT OF THE BOHEMIANS *Papus*		7.00
_____ WAYS TO SELF-REALIZATION *Mouni Sadhu*		7.00
_____ WITCHCRAFT, MAGIC & OCCULTISM—A Fascinating History *W. B. Crow*		7.00
_____ WITCHCRAFT—THE SIXTH SENSE *Justine Glass*		7.00
_____ WORLD OF PSYCHIC RESEARCH *Hereward Carrington*		2.00

SELF-HELP & INSPIRATIONAL

_____ CHARISMA How To Get "That Special Magic" *Marcia Grad*		7.00
_____ DAILY POWER FOR JOYFUL LIVING *Dr. Donald Curtis*		5.00
_____ DYNAMIC THINKING *Melvin Powers*		5.00
_____ GREATEST POWER IN THE UNIVERSE *U. S. Andersen*		7.00
_____ GROW RICH WHILE YOU SLEEP *Ben Sweetland*		7.00
_____ GROWTH THROUGH REASON *Albert Ellis, Ph.D.*		7.00
_____ GUIDE TO PERSONAL HAPPINESS *Albert Ellis, Ph.D. & Irving Becker, Ed. D.*		7.00
_____ HANDWRITING ANALYSIS MADE EASY *John Marley*		5.00
_____ HANDWRITING TELLS *Nadya Olyanova*		7.00
_____ HELPING YOURSELF WITH APPLIED PSYCHOLOGY *R. Henderson*		2.00
_____ HOW TO ATTRACT GOOD LUCK *A. H. Z. Carr*		7.00
_____ HOW TO BE GREAT *Dr. Donald Curtis*		5.00
_____ HOW TO DEVELOP A WINNING PERSONALITY *Martin Panzer*		5.00
_____ HOW TO DEVELOP AN EXCEPTIONAL MEMORY *Young & Gibson*		5.00
_____ HOW TO LIVE WITH A NEUROTIC *Albert Ellis, Ph. D.*		5.00
_____ HOW TO OVERCOME YOUR FEARS *M. P. Leahy, M.D.*		3.00
_____ HOW TO SUCCEED *Brian Adams*		7.00
_____ HUMAN PROBLEMS & HOW TO SOLVE THEM *Dr. Donald Curtis*		5.00
_____ I CAN *Ben Sweetland*		7.00
_____ I WILL *Ben Sweetland*		3.00
_____ KNIGHT IN THE RUSTY ARMOR *Robert Fisher*		10.00
_____ LEFT-HANDED PEOPLE *Michael Barsley*		5.00
_____ MAGIC IN YOUR MIND *U. S. Andersen*		7.00

____	MAGIC OF THINKING BIG *Dr. David J. Schwartz*	3.00
____	MAGIC OF THINKING SUCCESS *Dr. David J. Schwartz*	7.00
____	MAGIC POWER OF YOUR MIND *Walter M. Germain*	7.00
____	MENTAL POWER THROUGH SLEEP SUGGESTION *Melvin Powers*	3.00
____	NEVER UNDERESTIMATE THE SELLING POWER OF A WOMAN *Dottie Walters*	7.00
____	NEW GUIDE TO RATIONAL LIVING *Albert Ellis, Ph.D. & R. Harper, Ph.D.*	7.00
____	PROJECT YOU *A Manual of Rational Assertiveness Training Paris & Casey*	6.00
____	PSYCHO-CYBERNETICS *Maxwell Maltz, M.D.*	5.00
____	PSYCHOLOGY OF HANDWRITING *Nadya Olyanova*	7.00
____	SALES CYBERNETICS *Brian Adams*	7.00
____	SCIENCE OF MIND IN DAILY LIVING *Dr. Donald Curtis*	7.00
____	SECRET OF SECRETS *U. S. Andersen*	7.00
____	SECRET POWER OF THE PYRAMIDS *U. S. Andersen*	7.00
____	SELF-THERAPY FOR THE STUTTERER *Malcolm Frazer*	3.00
____	SUCCESS-CYBERNETICS *U. S. Andersen*	7.00
____	10 DAYS TO A GREAT NEW LIFE *William E. Edwards*	3.00
____	THINK AND GROW RICH *Napoleon Hill*	7.00
____	THINK YOUR WAY TO SUCCESS *Dr. Lew Losoncy*	5.00
____	THREE MAGIC WORDS *U. S. Andersen*	7.00
____	TREASURY OF COMFORT *edited by Rabbi Sidney Greenberg*	7.00
____	TREASURY OF THE ART OF LIVING *Sidney S. Greenberg*	7.00
____	WHAT YOUR HANDWRITING REVEALS *Albert E. Hughes*	3.00
____	YOUR SUBCONSCIOUS POWER *Charles M. Simmons*	7.00
____	YOUR THOUGHTS CAN CHANGE YOUR LIFE *Dr. Donald Curtis*	7.00

SPORTS

____	BICYCLING FOR FUN AND GOOD HEALTH *Kenneth E. Luther*	2.00
____	BILLIARDS—Pocket • Carom • Three Cushion *Clive Cottingham, Jr.*	5.00
____	CAMPING-OUT 101 Ideas & Activities *Bruno Knobel*	2.00
____	COMPLETE GUIDE TO FISHING *Vlad Evanoff*	2.00
____	HOW TO IMPROVE YOUR RACQUETBALL *Lubarsky Kaufman & Scagnetti*	5.00
____	HOW TO WIN AT POCKET BILLIARDS *Edward D. Knuchell*	5.00
____	JOY OF WALKING *Jack Scagnetti*	3.00
____	LEARNING & TEACHING SOCCER SKILLS *Eric Worthington*	3.00
____	MOTORCYCLING FOR BEGINNERS *I. G. Edmonds*	3.00
____	RACQUETBALL FOR WOMEN *Toni Hudson, Jack Scagnetti & Vince Rondone*	3.00
____	RACQUETBALL MADE EASY *Steve Lubarsky, Rod Delson & Jack Scagnetti*	5.00
____	SECRET OF BOWLING STRIKES *Dawson Taylor*	5.00
____	SECRET OF PERFECT PUTTING *Horton Smith & Dawson Taylor*	5.00
____	SOCCER—The Game & How to Play It *Gary Rosenthal*	5.00
____	STARTING SOCCER *Edward F. Dolan, Jr.*	5.00

TENNIS LOVERS' LIBRARY

____	BEGINNER'S GUIDE TO WINNING TENNIS *Helen Hull Jacobs*	2.00
____	HOW TO IMPROVE YOUR TENNIS—Style, Strategy & Analysis *C. Wilson*	2.00
____	PSYCH YOURSELF TO BETTER TENNIS *Dr. Walter A. Luszki*	2.00
____	TENNIS FOR BEGINNERS, *Dr. H. A. Murray*	2.00
____	TENNIS MADE EASY *Joel Brecheen*	5.00
____	WEEKEND TENNIS—How to Have Fun & Win at the Same Time *Bill Talbert*	3.00
____	WINNING WITH PERCENTAGE TENNIS—Smart Strategy *Jack Lowe*	2.00

WILSHIRE PET LIBRARY

____	DOG OBEDIENCE TRAINING *Gust Kessopulos*	5.00
____	DOG TRAINING MADE EASY & FUN *John W. Kellogg*	3.00
____	HOW TO BRING UP YOUR PET DOG *Kurt Unkelbach*	2.00
____	HOW TO RAISE & TRAIN YOUR PUPPY *Jeff Griffen*	5.00

*The books listed above can be obtained from your book dealer or directly from
Melvin Powers. When ordering, please remit $1.00 postage for the first book
and 50¢ for each additional book.*

Melvin Powers

12015 Sherman Road, No. Hollywood, California 91605